D0039243

Chambers
Pocket Guide to
Good Spelling

Compiled by George W. Davidson

Chambers

ISBN 0 550 18031 1

British Library Cataloguing in Publication Data

Davidson, George W.
    Chambers pocket guide to good spelling.
    1. Spellers
    I. Title
    428.1   PE1145.2
    ISBN 0-550-18031-1

Printed in Singapore by Singapore National Printers (Pte) Ltd.

Chambers

Pocket Guide to Good Spelling

Contents

Preface

To many people, English spelling seems infuriatingly
inconsistent and unpredictable, full of pitfalls and
uncertainties. *Harass* is spelt with one *r*, but *embarrass* with
two; the vowels of *speak* and *speech* are spelt differently, as are
those of *seize* and *siege*. The endings *-ance* and *-ence*, *-able* and
-ible, and *-tion* and *-sion* cause many headaches, as do words
like *guard* and *gauge*, *accommodation* and *accumulate*,
mischievous, *publicly*, and *professor*. Even good spellers have to
check the spelling of some word or other from time to
time—few people would claim never to make a spelling
mistake and many of us have 'blind spots' such as *separate*
which, try as we will, we can never be sure we have spelt
correctly.

Of course, the spelling of a word can always be checked in
an ordinary dictionary, but a dictionary does not explain
the rules of English spelling nor does it suggest ways of
remembering the correct spellings of words once they have
been checked. It is for this reason that W & R Chambers
have produced this *Pocket Guide to Good Spelling*, in which
users will find not only check-lists showing the correct
spelling of words which are commonly misspelt or confused
with each other, but also warnings about likely errors,
memory aids to help them remember the correct spellings
once they have found them, and clear explanations of the
rules of English spelling which will enable them to spell
correctly thousands of other words not themselves listed in
the check-lists.

This book is, in short, for everyone who wants to be sure
that their spelling is completely correct all of the time.
Students and secretaries in particular will find it an
invaluable companion in their work.

Introduction

The information in the *Pocket Guide to Good Spelling* is, for convenience, divided into seven chapters, each dealing with a different aspect of English spelling.

Chapter 1 comprises a list of a thousand of the most frequently misspelt English words, indicating where errors are likely to be made and often providing a memory aid to help the user remember the correct spelling in future. Another important feature of the entries in this chapter are the cross-references (marked with a double-headed arrow ⟹) to the sections in chapter 4 in which the most important rules of English spelling are fully explained, so relating the correct spelling of particular words to the general spelling-rules of English—another useful memory aid.

Chapter 2 lists words which are similar in sound and/or spelling and which are therefore sometimes misspelt or confused with each other. The differences between the words are clearly indicated by definitions and examples, and again memory aids and cross-references to general spelling-rules have been added wherever appropriate to help the user keep the distinctions in mind once they have been grasped.

For people who are not sure whether it is all right to write *alright*, and who are uncertain about the difference between *altogether* and *all together*, these and similar problems are explained in chapter 3, *One Word or Two?*, which deals with the spelling of words and phrases which sound alike.

The general rules of English spelling are explained in chapter 4. These have been listed in alphabetical order according to the topic covered, such as **-ance**, **-ence** (where the rules on spelling words such as *appearance*, *preference* and *occurrence* are explained), **-os, -oes** (covering the correct plural forms of nouns ending in **-o**), **abbreviations**, **capital letters**, **doubling of final consonants** (as in *hop : hopping, grit : gritty*, and so on) and **-dge** (in which the rules governing the spelling of words such as *judgement* and *fledgling* are explained).

Following this chapter on the main spelling-rules of English, the user is provided in chapter 5, *Beginnings, Middles and Endings*, with a check-list of the most frequent combining-elements from which English words are built up, such as **aero** (as in *aeroplane* and *aerodrome*), **sci** (as in *conscience* and *omniscience*) and **itis** (as in *bronchitis*). Learning the spelling of these elements will help with the correct spelling of many hundreds of words.

One problem many poor spellers face is finding a word in the dictionary when they do not know how to spell it in the first place. There would be little point in looking for *psychology* under *s* or *physical* under *f*. To help overcome this difficulty, chapter 6 provides a handy list of all the common spellings for the vowel and consonant sounds of English. If the user of this guide has searched for a word in a dictionary or word-list and has failed to find it, they should consult this list, and look for the word under some of the other spellings suggested. For example, if a user who has failed to find the words *knapsack* and *pneumatic* under the letter *n* consults the list, they will find that there are four other possible spellings for the beginnings of such words: *kn*, *gn*, *pn* and *mn*. If they then consult a dictionary at *kn*, *gn*, etc. in turn, they will of course find *knapsack* at *kn* and *pneumatic* at *pn*.

Although the emphasis throughout this book is on British English, differences between British and American usage have been indicated in various sections. In addition to these notes, some general comments on American spelling are to be found in chapter 7.

The seven chapters of this *Pocket Guide* thus cover all the main aspects of English spelling. In it users will find the answers to the thorny spelling problems which cause so many headaches for so many people.

Pronunciation guide

Accented syllables are shown by putting a stress mark after the accented syllable, thus *ban′dit*, *dis-pel′*, *dis-gust′ing*.

Vowels and diphthongs

Sound		Examples	Pronunciation
ā	as in fate, bare	name, hair	*nām, hār*
ä	as in father, far	grass, harm	*gräs, härm*
a	as in sat	bad, have	*bad, hav*
ē	as in me, fear	lean, here	*lēn, hēr*
e	as in pet	red, said	*red, sed*
ə	as in dinner	river, above	*riv′ər, ə-buv′*
ī	as in mine, sire	side, hire	*sīd, hīr*
i	as in bid	pin, busy	*pin, biz′i*
ō	as in mote	bone	*bōn*
ö	as in sport	board	*börd*
o	as in got	shot, shone	*shot, shon*
ōō	as in moon, poor	fool, tour	*fōōl, tōōr*
ŏŏ	as in foot	full, would	*fŏŏl, wŏŏd*
ū	as in mute, pure	tune, endure	*tūn, in-dūr′*
u	as in bud	run, love	*run, luv*
û	as in her	heard, bird, world, absurd	*hûrd, bûrd, wûrld, əb-sûrd′*
oi	as in boy	buoy, soil	*boi, soil*
ow	as in now	bough	*bow*

Consonants

b, d, f, h, j, k, l, m, n, p, r, s, t, v, w, and *z* are pronounced as in standard English.

The following other symbols are used:

Sound		Examples	Pronunciation
ch	as in cheap	church	*chûrch*
g	as in good	game	*gām*
sh	as in shine	shape, sugar	*shāp, shŏŏg′ər*
th	as in thin	theme, health	*thēm, helth*
dh	as in then	though, bathe	*dhō, bādh*
y	as in yet	yellow	*yel′ō*
zh	as in azure	pleasure	*plezh′ər*
ng	as in sing	wrong, sank	*rong, sangk*

1.

1000 Frequently Misspelt Words

The following list contains words which poor spellers frequently misspell, with the user's attention being drawn to the particular difficulties or pitfalls in each case. Cross-references marked with an arrow (⇒) are to the entries in chapter 4, *The General Rules of English Spelling*, where full explanations of the rules are given.

abandoned, abandoning   Do not double the final *n* when adding *-ed* and *-ing* ⇒ **doubling of final consonants.**

abattoir   One *b* and two *t*'s, as in *beef* and *mutton*.

abbreviate, abbreviation   Do not 'abbreviate' these words by omitting one of the *b*'s.

abhorrent   Note the double *r* and the *e*.

abominable   The *i* in the third syllable is sometimes slurred in speech; it must not be omitted in writing.

abscess   Note the *sc* in the middle of this word.

absence, absent, absentee   Notice the single *s* in the middle of these words. As a memory aid, remember that if you are *absent*, you may be *sent* for.

abysmal, abysmally   Note the spelling *bys* of the second syllable. Notice also the double *l* in *abysmally* ⇒ **-ly.**

academy   Note the *e* of the third syllable. As a memory aid, think of *academic* or the poetic word *academe*. Plural *academies* ⇒ **-y.**

accede   Note the ending *cede* ⇒ **-cede, -ceed, -sede.**

accelerate, accelerator   Note the single *l* and the *e* of the third syllable. Notice also that *accelerator* ends in *or* ⇒ **-er, -or, -ar.**

accessory   The *ory* spelling is now standard; the spelling *ary* is used only in legal phrases such as *an accessary after the fact*. Plural *accessories* ⇒ **-y.**

accidentally   Do not omit the *al*: the *ly* adverb ending is added to the adjective *accidental* to form this word.

accommodate, accommodation   Note the double *c* and double *m*.

accumulate, accumulation, accumulator   Two *c*'s but only one *m* and one *l* in these words. Notice also that *accumulator* ends in *or* ⇒ **-er, -or, -ar.**

accuracy, accurate   Two *c*'s and one *r* in these words.

achieve, achievement   Note the *ie* spelling ⇒ **-ei-, -ie-.**

acknowledge   The 'core' of this word is *know*, but note the *c* before the *k*.

acknowledgement, acknowledgment.   Both correct, but the form with the *e* retained before -*ment* is now commoner.

acquaint, acquaintance   Do not forget the *c* before the *q*.

acquiescent   Note the *c* before the *q* and the *sc* in the middle.

acquire   Note the *c* before the *q*.

acquit, acquittal   Note the *c* before the *q*. Notice also the double *t* in *acquittal* ⇒ **doubling of final consonants.**

acquisitive   Like *acquire*, this word has a *c* before the *q*. Note also the spelling *sit*; as a memory aid think of the related word *acquisitions*.

across   There is only one *c* in this word: to go *across* the street means the same as to *cross* the street.

address   Note the two *d*'s.

adequacy, adequate   Points to note in these words are the single *d*, the following *e* and the endings *acy* and *ate*.

adolescence, adolescent   Note the *sc* in these words, and the *en*.

advertise, advertisement   These words must always be spelt -*ise*, <u>never</u> -*ize* ⇒ **-ise, -ize.**

advise   Must always be spelt -*ise*, <u>never</u> -*ize* ⇒ **-ise, -ize.**

aerial   Note the *ae*.

aeroplane Note the *ae*; *airplane* is correct in American English, but not in British English.

aerosol Note the *ae*.

affiliate, affiliation Note the double *f* and single *l* in these words.

aggravate, aggravating Note the double *g* in these words.

aggression, aggressive These words have two *g*'s and two *s*'s.

aghast This word is related to *ghastly* and *ghost*, and like them has an *h* after the *g*.

align, alignment Take care with these words. They are connected in meaning with *line*, but being derived from French follow the French spelling, *ligne*.

allege, allegation Note the double *l*. If in doubt about the *g* of *allege*, think of *allegation*; if in doubt about the *e* of *allegation*, think of *allege*.

almond Note the *l*.

amateur Note the single *m* and the *eur*.

anaesthetic Note the *ae*.

analyse, analysis, analyst Note the *y* in these words. Note also that *analyse* must be spelt with an *s* in British English, never *z* ⟹ **-ise, -ize.**

annihilate, annihilation Note the double *n*, the *h* and the single *l*.

anonymous Note the *y*.

answer Take care not to omit the *w*. Knowing that *answer* is related to the word *swear* may serve as a memory aid.

Antarctic A common error is to omit the *c* between the *r* and the *t*.

antibiotic *Anti-* has the meaning 'against' here, therefore *anti-* is correct ⟹ **ante-, anti-.**

anticlimax This means 'the opposite of climax', so *anti-* is correct ⟹ **ante-, anti-.**

apartheid Note the *h* and the *ei*.

apologise, apology Points to note are the single *p* and the *log*. *Apologise* may also correctly be spelt *apologize* ⇒ **-ise, -ize.**

appalling Note the double *p* and the double *l*. For the doubling of the *l* of *appal* before *-ing* ⇒ **doubling of final consonants.**

apparent Note the double *p* and the *e*.

appearance Double *p*, but *a* in the final syllable.

appreciate, appreciation Note the double *p*.

aquarium Note that there is <u>no</u> *c* in this word.

arbitrary The third syllable of this word is sometimes slurred in speech. Take care when writing it.

architect, architecture Note the *ch* in these words.

Arctic As with *Antarctic*, the *c* between the *r* and the *t* is often omitted in speech. Take care to get the spelling correct in writing.

argument Note that the *e* of *argue* is dropped before *-ment*, contrary to the general rule (⇒ **-e**).

ascertain Note the *sc*. Memory aid: you try to *as̲c̲ertain* something because you want to be *as̲ c̲ertain* as possible about it.

asphyxiate, asphyxiation Note the *ph* and the *y*.

aspirin The *i* of the second syllable is often omitted in speech; take care not to do so in writing.

arthritis Note the *r* after *a*, sometimes omitted in speech.

assassin, assassinate Note the double *s*'s and the single *n*.

assistance, assistant These words have an *a* in the ending, contrary to what you might expect ⇒ **-ance, -ence.**

asthma Note the *th* in this word.

atheist Take care with the *ei*, and make sure you do not write 'athiest'.

attach No *t* before the *ch* ⇒ **-ch, -tch.**

autumn Note the final *n*, silent in *autumn*, but pronounced in *autumnal*. No capital needed for the names of seasons.

awful, awfully   Note that there is no *e* in these words, an exception to the general rule (⇒ **-e**).

bachelor   There is no *t* in this word!

baggage   Note the two *g*'s in the middle of this word.

baptise, baptize   Both correct ⇒ **-ise, -ize.**

basically   Do not omit the *al* from this word ⇒ **-ly.**

battalion   Two *t*'s and one *l*, as in *battle.*

beautiful, beautifully   Take care with the spelling *eau*, and note also the *fully* of the adverb which is often not fully pronounced in speech.

beggar   This is one of the few 'doer' words which end in *ar* ⇒ **-er, -or, -ar.**

beginner, beginning   Note the double *n* ⇒ **doubling of final consonants.**

belief, believe   Note the *ie* ⇒ **-ei-, -ie-.**

belligerent   Note the double *l* and the *g.*

beneficial   Note the *c* in this word.

benefited, benefiting   Do not double the *t* of *benefit* before adding *-ed* and *-ing* ⇒ **doubling of final consonants.**

besiege   Note the *ie* ⇒ **-ei-, -ie-.**

bias   Plural *biases*, but the verb parts are correct with a single or doubled *s*: *biases* or *biasses*, etc.

biscuit   Do not forget the *u*. Memory aid: *cuit* in this word means 'cooked', and comes from the same root as French *cuisine* (= cooking).

bizarre   Note the single *z* and double r.

blancmange   The French origins of this word (*blanc* = white, *manger* = to eat) are reflected in its spelling.

blasphemous, blasphemy   Note the *ph.*

boulder   A *u* is needed in this word if it means 'a rock or stone'; **bolder** means 'more bold'.

boundary   Note the ending *ary.*

bouquet   Note the *ou, qu* and *et.*

bourgeois   Note the *ou, ge* and *ois*.

boutique   Note the *ou,* the *i*, and the *que*.

boycott   Ends in two *t*'s.

braise   Spelt with an *s*, not a *z* ⟹ **-ise, -ize**.

brassière   This is the correct spelling of the word of which *bra* is the common contracted form. Note the double *s* and the accent on the *e*.

breadth   Note the *a* in this word.

breathalyse, breathalyser   These words are formed from *breath* and *analyse*, and like *analyse* they must always be spelt with an *s*, not a *z*.

brief   Note the *ie* ⟹ **-ei-, -ie-**.

brigadier   Note the ending *ier*.

Britain, British, Briton   There is only a single *t* in these words, but **Brittany** (in France) has a double *t*. Do not confuse the country *Britain* with *Briton*, an inhabitant of the country.

broccoli   Double *c*, single *l*.

brochure   Watch the spelling: *ch*, although pronounced [*sh*].

bronchitis   Note the *ch*.

bruise   Note the *ui* and the *s*.

brusque   Note the *que*.

Buddha, Buddhism, Buddhist   Note the double *d*, and in particular notice the position of the *h* in these words.

bulletin   Double *l*, single *t*.

buoyancy, buoyant   Like the *buoy* that floats in the sea, these words have a *u* before the *o*.

bureau   Note the *eau*. Plural *bureaux* or *bureaus* ⟹ **-x, -s**.

bureaucracy, bureaucratic   Note the *eau*, as in *bureau*, and the *-acy* ending of *bureaucracy* ⟹ **-acy, -asy**.

burglar, burglary   *Burglar* is one of the few 'doer' words which end in *ar* ⟹ **-er, -or, -ar**.

bus   Plural *buses*, verb-forms *buses*, *bused*, *busing*. Forms with double *s* are correct, but rare.

business   Do not forget the *i*, although it is not pronounced. Memory aid: this word is spelt as if it was formed from the adjective *busy*, which historically it is (⇒ **-y**); in present-day English, the '-ness' noun formed from *busy* is spelt *busyness*.

caffeine   Note the *ei* ⇒ **-ei-, -ie-.**

calendar   *E* in the second syllable, *a* in the third, not the other way round. Memory aid: a *cal<u>e</u>nd<u>a</u>r* shows the days of the *y<u>ea</u>r.*

camouflage   Note the *ou.*

campaign   Note the *ai* and the *g.*

cancelled, cancelling, cancellation   Note that the *l* of *cancel* is doubled before *-ed*, *-ing* and *-ation* ⇒ **doubling of final consonants.**

canoe   Present participle *canoeing* ⇒ **-e.**

capsize   Always spelt with a *z* ⇒ **-ise, -ize.**

carburettor   Note the double *t*; *carburetter* is also correct, but the form ending in *or* is the more common.

career   One *r* only in the middle of this word.

caress   One *r* only in the middle of this word.

Caribbean   Note the single *r* and double *b.*

carriage   Two *r*'s.

cashier   Note the ending *ier.*

casual, casually, casualty   Note the *ua.*

catarrh   One *t*, and note also the ending *rrh* (signifying 'running, flowing' as also in *diarrhoea* and *haemorrhage*).

ceiling   Note the *ei* ⇒ **-ei-, -ie-.**

cemetery   Do not omit the *e* of the third syllable, usually not pronounced in speech.

changeable   Note that the *e* of *change* is not dropped before *-able* ⇒ **-able, -ible.**

character   Note the initial *ch*.

characteristically   Note the ending *ally*. Do not omit the *al* ⇒ **-ly.**

chasm   Note the initial *ch*.

chauffeur   Note the *au*, double *f*, and *eu*.

chief, chiefly   Note the *ie* ⇒ **-ei-, -ie-.**

chilblain   Notice that one *l* of *chill* is dropped in this compound noun.

chimney   Plural *chimneys* ⇒ **-y.**

chocolate   Do not forget the second *o* of this word, often not pronounced in speech.

chronically   Note the initial *ch*. Note also the *al* before the *ly* ⇒ **-ly.**

cocoa   Note the final *oa*.

coconut   Notice that this is <u>not</u> *cocoanut*: *cocoa* and *coconuts* come from quite different plants.

collaborate, collaborator   Two *l*'s, one *b*. To *collaborate* is to 'work with someone', the core of the word being the same as in *laborious* and *laboratory*, and the *col-* being a form of the Latin word for 'with'. Note also that *collaborator* ends in *or* ⇒ **-er, -or, -ar.**

collapsible   Note the double *l*, and also the ending *-ible* ⇒ **-able, -ible.**

college   Note the ending *ege*.

colossal   Single *l*, followed by a double *s*. Memory aid: a firm that makes *colossal losses* may go bankrupt.

commemorate   Two *m*'s, then a single *m*. The core of this word is the same as that of *memory* and *memorial*, to which *com* is added.

commitment   Do not double the *t* of *commit* when it is followed by a suffix (or 'word-ending') beginning with a consonant ⇒ **doubling of final consonants.**

committed, committing   Note that the *t* of *commit* is doubled before *-ed* and *-ing* are added ⇒ **doubling of final consonants.**

committee Two *m*'s, two *t*'s, and two *e*'s. This word derives from the verb *commit*, and as with *committed* and *committing*, the *t* is doubled before the suffix *-ee* is added ⇒ **doubling of final consonants.**

comparative Note the a of the third syllable. Memory aid: if you think something is *comparatively* good, you *rate* it more highly than something else.

comparison Note the *i* of the third syllable: there is a difference in spelling between *comparison* and *comparative*.

compatible *-ible*, not *-able* ⇒ **-able, -ible.**

competitive, competitor If in doubt about the *i* of the third syllable, think of the related word *competition*, in which the *i* is clearly pronounced. Note also that *competitor* is one of the 'doer' words which end in *-or* ⇒ **-er, -or, -ar.**

complexion Note the *x* ⇒ **-ction, -xion.**

concede Note the spelling of *cede* ⇒ **-ceed, -cede, -sede.**

conceit, conceited *Ei*, not *ie* ⇒ **-ei-, -ie-.**

conceive *Ei*, not *ie* ⇒ **-ei-, -ie-.**

conference Note the *e* of the second syllable, often slurred in speech. Note also the single *r* ⇒ **doubling of final consonants.**

connection This is the usual spelling of this word, although *connexion* is also correct ⇒ **-ction, -xion.**

connoisseur This word is full of potential pitfalls! Note the double *n*, *oi*, double *s*, and *eur*.

conscience As an aid to spelling, notice that the core of this word is *science*, although the pronunciation is different.

conscientious This word is related to *conscience*, but note that *c* of *conscience* changes to *t* in *conscientious*, as in *science* and *scientific*.

conscious Note the *sci* in this word, as in *conscience* and *conscientious*.

contemporary The end of this word is often slurred in speech; note the spelling *orary*.

controversial Note *contro*, not *contra*: as a memory aid, think of *controversy*.

convalescence, convalescent Note the *val*, the *sc*, and the *en*.

convertible *-ible*, not *-able* ⟹ **-able, -ible.**

coolly The ending *-ly* is added to the adjective *cool*, therefore there is a double *l*.

coronary Some people tend to write this word with three *o*'s; note that the third syllable has an *a* in it. Memory aid: *coronary* and *heart* both have *ar* in them.

correspondence, correspondent Note the double *r*, and the *en*.

counterfeit *Ei*, not *ie* ⟹ **-ei-, -ie-.**

courageous The *e* of *courage* is retained in order to keep the *g* 'soft' (i.e. pronounced [*j*]).

courteous Note the *e* in this word, as also in **courtesy.**

critically The suffix *-ly* is added to the adjective *critical*, hence the ending *-ally*.

crochet, crocheted, crocheting The word *crochet* is taken from French, hence the *ch* spelling of a [*sh*] sound and the unpronounced final *t*.

crucifixion Note the *x* in this word ⟹ **-ction, -xion.**

cruelly The suffix *-ly* is added to the adjective *cruel*, hence the double *l*.

cryptic Note the *y*.

currency Note the double *r* and the *en*. Plural *currencies* ⟹ **-y.**

curriculum Only the *r* is doubled, the other consonants are all single letters.

cylinder Note the *cy* and the *er*.

cygnet (= a young swan). Note the *cy*.

Czech, Czechoslovakia *-slovakia* presents few problems, but *Czech* and *Czecho-* are sometimes misspelt: note the *cz*.

daffodil Double *f*, single *d* and *l*.

deceit, deceitful, deceive   *E* before *i* in these words, because following a *c* ⇒ **-ei-, -ie-.**

December   The first syllable of this word is sometimes misspelt. As a memory aid, remember that *December* was once the *tenth* month of the year, and the root of the word is the same as that in *decade* (= ten years).

decide, decision, decisive   Note the *dec* of these words.

defence, defensive   Note the *c* in the noun, and the *s* in the adjective. *Defense* is correct in American English, but incorrect in British English.

defendant   Note the ending *-ant* ⇒ **-ance, -ence.**

definite, definitely   Do not forget the *i* of the second syllable, often slurred in speech. As a memory aid, remember *definition* and *definitive*.

deliberate   Note the *de* and the *be*. If in doubt about the *ate*, think of *deliberation*.

demeanour   Note the *our* ending ⇒ **-or, -our.**

deodorant   Notice that the *u* of *odour* drops before the *ant* ⇒ **-or, -our.**

dependant, dependent   *Ant* is the correct ending for the noun, *ent* for the adjective ⇒ **-ance, -ence.** Note also the spelling of the noun **dependence.**

derelict   Note the spelling *rel*.

descend, descendant   Note the *sc*. Like *dependant*, the noun *descendant* ends in *ant* ⇒ **-ance, -ence.**

describe, description   Note the *des*.

desiccated   One *s* and two *c*'s, not the other way round as some people think: remember *desiccated coconut*.

despair   Note the *des*: if in doubt, think of *desperation*.

despatch see **dispatch.**

desperate   Note the *per*, often slurred in speech. If in doubt about the spelling *ate*, think of *desperation*.

despise   Note the spelling *des*. *Despise* must always be spelt *-ise*, never *-ize* ⇒ **-ise, -ize.**

detach, detached   There is no *t* before the *ch* in these words.

deterrent   Note the double *r* ⇒ **doubling of final consonants.**

develop   There is no *e* at the end of this word.

developed, developing   Do not double the *p* of *develop* before adding *-ed* and *-ing* ⇒ **doubling of final consonants.**

development   As there is no *e* at the end of *develop*, there is no *e* between the *p* and *m* in *development*.

diamond   Do not forget the *a* in this word.

diaphragm   Note the *ph* and the silent *g*.

diarrhoea   Note the *rrh* (which has its origins in a Greek word meaning 'to run, flow' —compare *catarrh* and *haemorrhage*), and the *oe*.

difference, different   Do not forget the *e* of the second syllable, often slurred in speech.

dilemma   One *l*, two *m*'s.

dilettante   One *l*, two *t*'s.

diligence, diligent   Note the spelling *lig*.

diphtheria   Note the *ph*.

disappear, disappearance   One *s* and two *p*'s, as formed from *dis-* plus *appear(ance)*.

disappoint   One *s* and two *p*'s, as formed from *dis-* plus *appoint*.

disapprove, disapproval   One *s* and two *p*'s, as formed from *dis-* plus *approve/approval*.

disastrous   One *s* in *dis*, and notice that the *e* of *disaster* is dropped before the ending *ous*.

disc, disk   Both spellings are correct; *disc* is the more common spelling, except in the field of computer science where *disk* is more frequently used.

discipline, disciplinary   Note the *sc*, and the ending *ary*.

discourteous   Note the *ou* and the *e*.

discrepancy Note the *an*. Plural *discrepancies* ⟹ **-y.**

dishevelled Note the double *l*.

disk see **disc.**

dispatch, despatch Both correct; *dis* is the commoner.

dissatisfaction Double *s*, as formed from *dis-* plus *satisfaction*. Similarly with **dissatisfied.**

dissect Contrary to what the pronunciation would lead you to expect, there is a double *s* in this word.

dissent Note the double *s* in this word.

dissimilar Formed from *dis-* plus *similar*, therefore double *s*.

dissolve Note the double *s*, contrary to what the pronunciation might lead one to expect.

divide, division Note the *div*.

donkey Plural *donkeys* ⟹ **-y.**

don'ts Note the position of the apostrophe.

doubt, doubtful Note the silent *b*.

drunkenness Formed from *drunken* plus the suffix *-ness*, therefore a double *n*.

dryer, drier Both correct for the noun, *drier* alone correct for the comparative adjective ⟹ **-y.**

dryly, drily Both correct ⟹ **-y.**

duly Notice that the *e* of *due* is dropped in *duly*, contrary to what one would expect from the general rule ⟹ **-e.**

dutiful The *y* of *duty* changes to *i* before the suffix *-ful* ⟹ **-y.**

earnest Note the *ear*.

earring Formed from *ear* plus *ring*, therefore double *r*.

eccentric Note the double *c*.

ecstasy Note the *cs* and the ending *asy*.

eczema Note the *cz*.

eerily, eeriness Contrary to the general rule (⟹ **-e**), the *e* of *eerie* drops in *eerily* and *eeriness*.

effervescence Note the double *f*, the *sc*, and the *en*.

eighth   Notice that there is only one *t* in this word, although the pronunciation would lead you to expect two.

elegance, elegant   Note the *leg* and the *an*.

eligible, eligibility   Note the *lig*; also the *-ible/-ibility* ⟹ **-able, -ible.**

embarrass, embarrassment   Note the double *r* and double *s*. Warning: notice the difference in spelling between *embarrass* and *harass*. Memory aid: you might go *really red* with *embarrassment*.

encyclopaedia, encyclopedia   Both correct, but *ae* still commoner in British English ⟹ **-ae-, -e-.**

endeavour   Note the *ea*, and the *ou* ⟹ **-or, -our.**

enquire see **inquire.**

enrol, enrolment   Note that there is only one *l* in these words. The *l* of *enrol* is doubled in *enrolled* and *enrolling* ⟹ **doubling of final consonants.**

enthusiastically   Note the ending *ally* ⟹ **-ly.**

envelope   There is an *e* at the end of the word for the folder into which one puts a letter.

equalise, equalize   Notice that the final *l* of a base word (in this case, *equal*) does not double before **-ise/-ize** ⟹ the section on *l* in **doubling of final consonants.**

erroneous   Double *r* as in *err* and *error.* Note also the ending *eous.*

etc.   A common error is to write *ect.* Take care.

etiquette   One *t* at the beginning, two *t*'s at the end.

exaggerate, exaggeration   Note the double *g.*

exasperate, exasperation   Note the *per.*

exceed, exceedingly   Note the *ceed* ⟹ **-cede, -ceed, -sede.**

excellence, excellent   Note the *c* after the *x*, the double *l* and the *en.*

excerpt   Note *c* after the *x*, and the *p* before the *t*, sometimes slurred in speech.

excise Can never be written with a z ⇒ **-ise, -ize.**

exciting A common mistake is to omit the *c*. Take care.

exercise Can never be written with a z ⇒ **-ise, -ize.**

exhaust, exhaustion Do not forget the *h* in these words.

exhibit, exhibition Do not forget the *h* in these words.

exhilarate, exhilaration Do not forget the *h* in these words. Note also the spelling *lar*; memory aid—the base of these words is the same as that in *hilarious* and *hilarity*, where the *a* is more clearly pronounced.

exhort, exhortation Do not forget the silent *h* in these words.

expense Note that this word ends in *se*.

extension Note the *s* in this word: if in doubt, think of *extensive*.

extraordinary Do not forget the *a* of *extra* in this word, usually slurred in speech.

extravagance, extravagant Note the *a*'s in *-vagance* and *-vagant*.

extravert, extrovert Both correct; the form with *a* is the commoner of the two.

façade Notice that this word, borrowed from French, should have a small hook-like mark, called a cedilla, under the *c*.

facetious Note the spelling of the ending, *ious*.

fallible *-ible*, not *-able* ⇒ **-able, -ible.**

family Do not omit the *i*, often slurred in speech. Plural *families* ⇒ **-y.**

fascinate, fascination Note the *sc*.

favourite Note the *ou*, often slurred in speech.

feasible *-ible*, not *-able* ⇒ **-able, -ible.**

February Take care with the spelling of *-ruary*, usually slurred in speech.

field *I* before *e* ⇒ **-ei-, -ie-.**

fiend *I* before *e* ⇒ **-ei-, -ie-.**

fierce   *I* before *e* ⇒ **-ei-, -ie-.**

fiery   *I* before *e* ⇒ **-ei-, -ie-.**

finish   There is only one *n* in this word.

fledgling   Note that the *e* of *fledge* is dropped before the suffix *-ling*, contrary to what one would expect from the general rule ⇒ **-dge.**

fluorescent   Note the *u* and the *sc.*

fluoride, fluoridation   Note the *u.*

focus   Noun plural *focuses*; verb-forms with single or double *s*, e.g. *focused, focussed* ⇒ **doubling of final consonants.**

foliage   Note the single *l.*

foreboding   *Fore-*, not *for-* ⇒ **for-, fore-.**

foreign, foreigner   Note the *ei* (⇒ **-ei-, -ie-**) and the silent *g.*

forfeit   Note the *ei* ⇒ **-ei-, -ie-.**

forgiveness   Only one *n*, exactly as the pronunciation would suggest.

forgo   *For-*, not *fore-*, precisely as the meaning 'do without' would suggest ⇒ **for-, fore-.**

forty   Note: this is <u>not</u> *fourty.*

frantically   Note the ending *ally* ⇒ **-ly.**

friend   *I* before *e* (⇒ **-ei-, -ie-**); if in doubt, remember that *fri<u>end</u>* ends in *<u>end</u>.*

frolic   Note the *k* in *frolicked* and *frolicking* ⇒ **-c.**

fulfil, fulfilment   Note the single *l*'s in these words.

fulfilled, fulfilling   The final *l* of *fulfil* is doubled before *-ed* and *-ing* ⇒ **doubling of final consonants.**

fulsome   Note the single *l* in this word.

fundamental   Note the *a* in the second syllable.

fuselage   Note the *e* of the second syllable.

gaiety, gaily   Note that the *y* of *gay* becomes *i* in these words.

galloped, galloping   The *p* is not doubled when *-ed* and *-ing* are added ⇒ **doubling of final consonants.**

gaol Watch the spelling of this word. If in doubt, use *jail*.

gas Noun plural *gases*, verb-forms *gasses, gassed, gassing* ⇒ **doubling of final consonants.**

gâteau Note the accent over the *a*, and the *eau*. Plural usually *gâteaux*, but *gâteaus* also correct ⇒ **-x, -s.**

gauge Take care to put the *u* in the correct place.

ghastly Watch the *h*.

ghetto Watch the *h*. Plural *ghettos* ⇒ **-os, -oes.**

ghost, ghostly Watch the *h*.

ghoul, ghoulish Watch the *h*.

gipsy see **gypsy.**

giraffe One *r*, two *f*'s.

glamorise, glamorous Note that the *u* of *glamour* is dropped before *-ise* and *-ous* ⇒ **-or, -our.** *Glamorise* may also be spelt with a *z* ⇒ **-ise, -ize.**

gluttonous, gluttony Two *t*'s, one *n*.

gorgeous Note the *e*.

gorilla One *r*, two *l*'s.

gossiping, gossipy The *p* of *gossip* does not double before a suffix ⇒ **doubling of final consonants.**

government The *n* of *govern* is not pronounced when *-ment* is added, but must not be omitted in writing.

governor Note that this ends in *or*.

graffiti Two *f*'s, one *t*.

grammar A common error is to write *er* instead of *ar*. As a memory aid, think of *grammatical*.

grandeur Note the spelling *eur*.

grateful Note the *ate*. This word is connected with *gratitude*.

gray, grey The preferred spelling in British English is *grey*; *gray* is also correct, and is standard in American English.

grief, grieve, grievance Note the *ie* ⇒ **-ei-, -ie-.**

grievous *I* before *e*, as in *grief* and *grieve*. Note that there is no *i* after the *v*—just follow the pronunciation, [$gr\bar{e}'vəs$], and you will not go wrong.

gruesome Do not forget the *e* of *grue*.

guarantee Note the *u* and the single *r*.

guard, guardian Note the *u*.

guerrilla Note the *u*, the double *r*, and the double *l*. A single *r* is also correct, but is less common.

guess Note the *u*.

guest Note the *u*.

guide, guidance Note the *u* in these words. Note also the ending *-ance* in *guidance* ⇒ **-ance, -ence.**

guilt, guilty Note the *u*.

gullible *-ible*, not *-able*, contrary to what one might expect from the general rule ⇒ **-able, -ible.**

gymkhana Note the *y* and the *kh*.

gypsy, gipsy Both correct, but the *y* spelling is the commoner. Plural *gypsies/gipsies* ⇒ **-y.**

haemorrhage Care should be taken with the *ae*, the single *m* and the *rrh* (the same *rrh* as is found in *catarrh* and *diarrhoea*).

handicapped Notice that the *p* of *handicap* is doubled before a suffix such as *-ed* ⇒ **doubling of final consonants.**

handkerchief Notice that this word begins with *hand*, although the *d* is usually slurred in speech. Notice also that the word ends in *chief*.

happened, happening Note the double *p*. The *n* is not doubled before *-ed* and *-ing* ⇒ **doubling of final consonants.**

harangue Note the single *r* and the final *ue*.

harass, harassment Single *r* and double *s*. Warning: note the difference in spelling between *harass* and *embarrass*. Memory aid: you may be *harassed harshly*.

hazard, hazardous Note the single *z*.

height   Although related to *high*, this word has an *e* in it ⇒ **-ei-, -ie-.**

heinous   Note the *ei* ⇒ **-ei-, -ie-.**

heir, heiress   Note the silent *h* and the *ei* ⇒ **-ei-, -ie-.**

herbaceous   Note the ending *eous*.

hereditary   Note the *a* of *ary*, often slurred in speech.

hero   Plural *heroes* ⇒ **-os, -oes.**

hiccup, hiccough   Both correct, but the first form is much to be preferred. Note that the *p* is not doubled before *-ed* and *-ing* i.e. *hiccuped, hiccuping* ⇒ **doubling of final consonants.**

hideous   Note the *e*.

hierarchy   Note the *ie* ⇒ **-ei-, -ie-.**

hieroglyphics   Note the *ie* (⇒ **-ei-, -ie-**), the *y* and the *ph*.

hindrance   Notice that the *e* of *hinder* is dropped in this word, as its pronunciation indicates.

honorary   Note the ending *ary*, often slurred in speech.

honourable   Notice that the *u* of *honour* is not dropped before the suffix *-able* ⇒ **-or, -our.**

horrible   Note the double *r*, and the ending *-ible*—if in doubt over choosing *-ible* or *-able*, think of *horrid* ⇒ **-able, -ible.**

humorous   Notice that the second *u* of *humour* is dropped before the suffix *-ous* ⇒ **-or, -our.**

Hungary   Note the *a* in this word; think of the related word *Hungarian*.

hygiene, hygienic   *Ie*, not *ei* ⇒ **-ei-, -ie-**; note also the *y*.

hypochondria, hypochrondriac   Note the *y* and the *ch*.

hypocrisy   Note the *y* of *hypo*, and particularly the *i* and the *s* of the ending. Memory aid: if in doubt about the *i*, think of *hypocritical*.

hypocrite   In addition to the points mentioned under *hypocrisy*, note also the final *e*.

hysterically   Note the *y* of the first syllable. Notice also the *ally*—the suffix *-ly* is added to the adjective *hysterical*.

idiosyncrasy Note the *y*, and particularly the ending *asy* (⇒ **-acy, -asy**). If in doubt about the *a*, think of *idiosyncratic*.

illegal This word is formed from *il-* (= 'not') and *legal*, hence the double *l*.

illegible This word is formed from *il-* (= 'not') and *legible*, hence the double *l*; *-ible*, not *-able* ⇒ **-able, -ible.**

illiterate This word is formed from *il-* (= 'not') and *literate*, hence the double *l*. Note also the single *t* in *lit*.

imaginary Note the *a* of the ending *ary*.

immediate, immediately Note the double *m*.

immense Note the double *m*.

immigrant, immigration This means 'a migrant, or migration, *in*to a country', hence the double *m*.

immoral This word is formed from *im-* (= 'not') and *moral*, hence the double *m*.

immortal This word is formed from *im-* (= 'not') and *mortal*, hence the double *m*.

impostor Note the *or* ending.

improvise Always *-ise*, never *-ize* ⇒ **-ise, -ize.**

inaccurate This word is formed from *in-* (= 'not') and *accurate*, therefore only one *n*; note also the double *c*, and the *ate* ending.

incidentally Note the *ally*: the suffix *-ly* is added to the adjective *incidental* to form this word.

incredible *-ible*, not *-able* ⇒ **-able, -ible.**

indefinitely Note the *fin* and the *ite*. As a memory aid, think of the word *finite*, where the *i*'s are clearly pronounced.

independent Note the *ent* ending, for the noun and the adjective. Warning: this is different from the spelling rule for *dependent/dependant*.

indestructible Note the ending *-ible* ⇒ **-able, -ible.**

indict, indictment Note the *c*'s in these words.

indifference, indifferent Note the syllable *fer*, often slurred in speech.

inexhaustible Note the silent *h*, and also the *-ible* ending ⟹ **-able, -ible.**

infallible *-ible*, not *-able* ⟹ **-able, -ible.**

inflammable Note the double *m*; *-able*, not *-ible* ⟹ **-able, -ible** (if in doubt, think of *inflammation*).

innocent Note the double *n*.

innumerable This word means 'so great as to be *not* (= *in-*) *numberable*', hence the double *n*.

inoculate, inoculation Note that there is only <u>one</u> *n* in these words. Note also the single *c* and *l*.

inquire, enquire, inquiry, enquiry Spellings with *in* and *en* are equally correct, although some people prefer to use *enquire/enquiry* when all that is meant is a simple asking, and *inquire/inquiry* when a more detailed investigation is meant.

inseparable Note the *par*. Memory aid: if people are *inseparable*, they are rarely *apart*.

install, instal Both correct, but the first form is the commoner ⟹ **-l, -ll.**

instalment Only one *l* in this word ⟹ **-l, -ll.**

instil Ends in a single *l* ⟹ **-l, -ll.**

interested, interesting Note the *e* of the second syllable, often slurred in speech.

interrogate, interrogation Note the double *r*.

interrupt, interruption Note the double *r*.

introduce, introduction Note the *o* of *intro*.

irascible Note the single *r*, as in *ire* and *irate*, and the *-ible* (⟹ **-able, -ible**).

irregular This word is formed from *ir-* (= 'not') and *regular*, hence the double *r*.

irrelevant Formed from *ir-* (= 'not') and *relevant*, hence the double *r*.

irresistible Formed from *ir-* (= 'not') and *resistible*, hence the double *r*; note also the ending *-ible* ⟹ **-able, -ible.**

irresponsible Formed from *ir-* (= 'not') and *responsible*, hence the double *r*. Note also the ending *-ible* ⟹ **-able, -ible.**

irritable, irritate, irritation Note the double *r*.

itinerary Note the spelling of the end of this word, *erary*, often slurred in speech.

jeopardise, jeopardy Note the *o*. *Jeopardise* may also be spelt *-ize* ⟹ **-ise, -ize.**

jersey Plural *jerseys* ⟹ **-y.**

jeweller Note that the *l* of *jewel* is doubled before the ending *-er* ⟹ **doubling of final consonants.**

jewellery, jewelry Both correct, but the first form is much the commoner in British English.

jockey Plural *jockeys* ⟹ **-y.**

jodhpurs The *h* is often incorrectly placed—note that it stands <u>between</u> the *d* and the *p*.

journey Plural *journeys* ⟹ **-y.**

judgement, judgment Both correct, but the former is now the commoner.

keenness Formed from *keen* plus *-ness*, hence the double *n*.

kidnapped, kidnapping, kidnapper Notice that the *p* of *kidnap* is doubled before a suffix, contrary to the general rules ⟹ **doubling of final consonants.**

kidney Plural *kidneys* ⟹ **-y.**

knowledgeable The final *e* of *knowledge* is retained before *-able* ⟹ **-dge.**

laboratory Note the spelling of the ending *atory*, often slurred in speech.

laborious Notice that the *u* of *labour* is dropped before the suffix *-ious* ⟹ **-or, -our.**

labyrinth Note the *y*, often slurred in speech.

lacquer Note the *c*, the *qu* and the *e*.

laid   The past tense of *lay* is an exception to the general rule governing the spelling of words ending in a vowel followed by *y* when a suffix is added ⇒ **-y.**

language   Note the position of the *u*, often incorrectly placed after the *a* although the pronunciation of the word gives a clear indication of where the *u* should be.

languor, languorous   Note the *u* after the *g* in these words. Memory aid: remember that these words are related to *languid*, in which the *u* is clearly pronounced.

laryngitis   Note the *y.*

lascivious   Note the *sc.*

launderette   The *e* of *launder* is retained in this word, although it is often slurred in speech; it is dropped in **laundry**, however.

leisure   *E* before *i* in this word ⇒ **-ei-, -ie-.**

leopard   Note the *o.*

liaise, liaison   One or other of the *i*'s is sometimes omitted in error; take particular care with the *iai.*

library   The middle syllable of this word is sometimes slurred in speech—note the *ary* ending. Memory aid: think of *librarian*, in which the *a* is clearly pronounced. Plural *libraries* ⇒ **-y.**

licence, license   *-ce* for the noun in British English, *-se* for the verb ⇒ **-ce, -se.**

lieutenant   Note the spelling of the first syllable of this word.

liquefy   Note the *e* in this word, one of the few words which end in *efy.*

liqueur   Note the *ueu.*

liquor   Note the *o.*

literate, literature   There is only a single *t* after the *i.*

longitude   By analogy with *latitude*, some people wrongly insert a *t* after the *long*, in speech and writing.

luggage   Like *baggage*, *luggage* has two *g*'s in the middle.

Madeira This is spelt *ei*, contrary to the general rule ⟹ **-ei-, -ie-.**

magnanimous Notice the *i* of *animous*: if in doubt, think of *magnanimity* in which the *i* is clearly pronounced.

maintenance Note the *e* of *ten*, and the ending *-ance*.

manageable The *e* of *manage* is retained before *-able* in order to keep the 'soft' [*j*] sound of the letter *g* ⟹ **-able, -ible.**

manoeuvre Note the *oeu*.

margarine Note that in spite of the 'soft' [*j*] sound of the letter *g*, the *g* is followed by an *a*.

marmalade Note the *a* of the second syllable.

marriage Do not forget the *i*: remember that this word is derived from *marry*, the *y* changing to an *i* before the suffix *-age*.

martyr Note the *y*.

marvellous The *l* of *marvel* is doubled before the suffix *-ous* ⟹ **doubling of final consonants.**

marzipan Note the *i*.

massacre Note the double *s*.

mayonnaise Note the double *n*.

medallist The *l* of *medal* is doubled before the suffix *-ist* ⟹ **doubling of final consonants.**

medicine Note the *i* of the second syllable. If in doubt, remember *medicinal*, in which the *i* is clearly pronounced.

medieval, mediaeval Both correct, but the form with *e* alone is now commoner in British English than that with *ae*, and is standard in American English.

Mediterranean Note the single *d* and *t*, and the double *r*. Memory aid: this word means 'in the middle of the land' —*Medi* is connected with *medium*, *terra* with *terrain* and *terrestrial*.

meringue The pronunciation of this word reflects its French origins, and so does its spelling—note the *i* and the final *ue*.

messenger   Note the *eng*.

meteorology, meteorologist, meteorological   Notice that the core of these words is *meteor*, although the *e* is often slurred in speech.

milage, mileage   Both correct.

millennium   Two *l*'s and two *n*'s. Memory aid: this word is based on root-words meaning 'a thousand' and 'years'; the same roots are found in *mil̲l̲imetre* and *an̲n̲ual*.

millionaire   Two *l*'s, but only one *n*.

miniature   Note the *a*.

ministry   The *e* of *minister* is dropped in this word.

minuscule   Note the *u* of the second syllable. It is a common error to write an *i* here: if in doubt, think of *min̲u̲te* (= 'tiny').

miraculous   Note the single *l*.

miscellaneous   Note the *sc*, the double *l* and the ending *eous*.

mischief, mischievous   *Ie*, not *ei* ⇒ **-ei-, -ie-**. Note that there is no *i* before the *ous* in *mischievous*: if in doubt, just follow the pronunciation.

misshapen   This word is formed from *mis-* (= 'badly') and *shape*, hence the double *s*.

misspell, misspelt   These words are formed from *mis-* (= 'badly') and *spell/spelt*, hence the double *s*.

misspent   This word is formed from *mis-* (= 'badly') and *spent*, hence the double *s*.

moccasin   Double *c*, single *s*.

monkey   Plural *monkeys* ⇒ **-y.**

mortgage   Note the *t*.

murderous   Notice that the *e* of *murder* is retained in this word, although often slurred in speech.

naïve, naive   It is equally correct to write this word with or without the diaeresis over the *i*. Related nouns are **naïvety** (with or without the diaeresis) or **naïveté** (the French form of the word preferred by some, from which the diaeresis should not be omitted).

necessary, necessity   One *c*, two *s*'s.

negligence, negligent   Points to take care over are the *i* and the -*ence* (⇒ **-ance, -ence**).

negligible   Note the -*ible* ending ⇒ **-able, -ible**.

Negro   Plural *Negroes* ⇒ **-os, -oes**.

neighbour   *Ei*, not *ie* ⇒ **-ei-, -ie-**.

neither   *Ei*, not *ie* ⇒ **-ei-, -ie-**.

niece   *I* before *e* in this word ⇒ **-ei-, -ie-**.

ninth   Note that the *e* of *nine* is dropped in this word.

noticeable   The *e* of *notice* is retained in order to preserve the 'soft' [*s*] sound of the letter *c* before the suffix -*able* ⇒ **-able, -ible**.

nuisance   Note the *ui* and the *ance*.

nutritious   Note the *i* before the *ous*.

obscene, obscenity   Note the *sc*.

obstreperous   Note the *per*.

occasion, occasional, occasionally   Two *c*'s, one *s*.

occupation, occupy   Two *c*'s, one *p*.

occur   Two *c*'s.

occurred, occurring, occurrence   Notice that the *r* of *occur* is doubled before a suffix ⇒ **doubling of final consonants**.

of   Often wrongly substituted for *have* in constructions like *He must have done it*.

offence, offensive   *C* in the noun, but *s* in the adjective.

offered, offering   The *r* of *offer* is <u>not</u> doubled before a suffix ⇒ **doubling of final consonants**.

omit, omission   Only one *m* in these words.

omitted, omitting   The *t* of *omit* is doubled before a suffix beginning with a vowel ⇒ **doubling of final consonants**.

opponent   Two *p*'s, one *n*.

opportunity   Two *p*'s.

opposite, opposition   Two *p*'s, one *s*.

ordinary   Note the *a*, often slurred in speech.

outrageous   The *e* of *outrage* is retained in order to preserve the 'soft' [*j*] sound of the *g* before the suffix *-ous*.

overrule   This word is formed from *over* and *rule*, therefore two *r*'s are necessary.

paid   The past tense of *pay* is an exception to the general rule governing the spelling of words ending in a vowel plus *y* when a suffix is added ⇒ **-y.**

panicked, panicking, panicky   A word ending in *c* usually adds a *k* before *-ed*, *-ing*, or *-y* ⇒ **-c.**

paraffin   One *r*, two *f*'s—remember that the discoverer of *paraffin* called it that because it has little chemical *affinity* for other substances.

parallel, paralleled, paralleling   Note the single *r*, the double *l* and the single *l*. Memory aid: a *pair* of *long lines* which *lie parallel*. Contrary to the general rule for words which end in *l* preceded by a single vowel (⇒ **doubling of final consonants**), the final *l* of *parallel* does <u>not</u> double before *-ed* and *-ing*.

paralyse, paralysis, paralytic   One *r*, one *l*, and note also the *y*. *Paralyse* may not be written with a *z* ⇒ **-ise, -ize.**

paraphernalia   Do not omit the *r* of *pher*.

parliament, parliamentary   Remember the *i* in these words.

passenger   Note the spelling *eng*.

peaceable   The *e* of *peace* is retained to preserve the 'soft' [*s*] sound of the *c* before the suffix *-able* ⇒ **-able, -ible.**

pendant   This noun ends in *ant*, just like *dependant* ⇒ **-ance, -ence.**

perceptible   *-ible*, not *-able* ⇒ **-able, -ible.**

perennial   One *r*, two *n*'s, just as in the Latin phrase *per annum*.

perilous   One *l* only in this word ⇒ **doubling of final consonants.**

permitted, permitting   The *t* of *permit* is doubled before a suffix such as *-ed* and *-ing* ⇒ **doubling of final consonants.**

persistence, persistent Note the endings *-ence* and *-ent* ⇒ **-ance, -ence.**

personnel There are two *n*'s in the word meaning 'staff, employees'.

Pharaoh Note the *aoh* at the end of this word.

phobia Note the initial *ph*.

physically Note the *ph* and the *y*, and especially the *ally*.

physique The pronunciation of the *i* and the final *que* reflect this word's French origins.

piano Plural *pianos* ⇒ **-os, -oes.**

picnicked, picnicker, picnicking *K* is generally added to a word ending in *c* before a suffix beginning with *e, i* or *y* ⇒ **-c.**

picturesque Note the *que*.

piece *I* before *e* in this word ⇒ **-ei-, -ie-.**

pigmy see **pygmy**.

plateau Plural *plateaux* or *plateaus* ⇒ **-x, -s.**

plausible *-ible*, not *-able* ⇒ **-able, -ible.**

playwright *Wright* here means 'a maker', as in *shipwright*. Do not be misled by the notion of 'writing'.

pneumonia Do not forget the initial silent *p*.

Portuguese Remember the *u* after the *g*.

possess, possession, possessive Two *s*'s twice over in these words.

possible, possibility Note the double *s* and the *ib* ⇒ **-able, -ible.**

posthumous Note the silent *h*.

potato Plural *potatoes* ⇒ **-os, -oes.**

practice, practise In British English, the noun is written with a *c*, the verb with an *s*.

precede Note the ending *cede* ⇒ **-cede, -ceed, -sede.**

predecessor One *c*, two *s*'s, and *or* at the end (⇒ **-er, -or, -ar**).

preferable One *r*, and *-able* ⇒ **-able, -ible.**

preference One *r* and *-ence* (⟹ **-ance, -ence**); if in doubt, remember *preferential*.

preferred, preferring The final *r* of *prefer* is doubled before *-ed* and *-ing* ⟹ **doubling of final consonants.**

preparation Note the *par*: remember the related verb *prepare* and adjective *preparatory*.

priest *I* before *e* in this word ⟹ **-ei-, -ie-.**

privilege Notice that this word does not end in *-dge*; note also the *i* of the second syllable.

probably Take care over the second syllable *bab*, often slurred in speech.

procedure Note the single *e* of the second syllable.

proceed Note the spelling *ceed* ⟹ **-cede, -ceed, -sede.**

profession, professional One *f*, two *s*'s.

professor One *f*, two *s*'s, and *or* at the end.

proffer This word is the only common [*prof*] word with a double *f*. It comes from the same Latin word as *offer*.

profitable, profited, profiting There is only one *f* in *profit*; the final *t* does not double before a suffix ⟹ **doubling of final consonants.**

program, programme *Programme* is the normal spelling in British English, *program* in American English. However, *program* is the spelling generally adopted in computer science. Note that whichever base form is used, the participles are *programming* and *programmed* ⟹ **doubling of final consonants.**

pronunciation Watch this word! It is related to the verb *pronounce*, but the spelling of *pronunciation* follows its pronunciation!

propellant The *l* of *propel* is doubled before a suffix. Note the *ant* ending for this noun, as with the nouns *dependant* and *pendant* ⟹ **-ance, -ence.**

propeller The *l* of *propel* is doubled before a suffix beginning with a vowel and the suffix in this case is *er* ⇒ **doubling of final consonants.**

prophecy, prophesy *Cy* for the noun, *sy* for the verb.

protein *Ei*, not *ie*—an exception to the general '*i* before *e*' rule ⇒ **-ei-, -ie-.**

psychiatry, psychiatrist, psychiatric These words have as their core *psych* (= 'mind'), as do **psychic, psychology, psychologist.** Note the spelling of the *psych* part of these words.

publicly This word is an exception to the general rule for forming adverbs from adjectives ending in *-ic* (⇒ **-ly**); note that *-ly* is added directly to *public.*

pursue, pursuit Note the spelling *pur.*

pygmy, pigmy Both correct, but *pyg* is preferred.

pyjamas Note the *y*: *pajamas* is correct only in American English.

pyramid Note the *y*.

querulous Only one *l*.

questionnaire All derivatives of *question* have a single *n* (e.g. *questioned*, *questionable*) except *questionnaire*, which has two.

quiz Plural *quizzes* ⇒ **doubling of final consonants.**

really This word is formed from *real* plus *-ly*, therefore two *l*'s are needed.

rebelled, rebelling, rebellion, rebellious The *l* of *rebel* is doubled before a suffix ⇒ **doubling of final consonants.**

recede Note the spelling *cede* ⇒ **-cede, -ceed, -sede.**

receipt *E* before *i* after the *c* (⇒ **-ei-, -ie-**), and do not forget the silent *p*.

receive *Ei* after the *c* ⇒ **-ei-, -ie-.**

recognise Do not omit the *g*, often slurred in speech. May also be spelt *-ize* ⇒ **-ise, -ize.**

recommend, recommendation One *c*, two *m*'s.

reconnaissance Two *n*'s, two *s*'s, and *ance*.

recurrence, recurrent The final *r* of *recur* is doubled before a suffix beginning with a vowel ⇒ **doubling of final consonants.**

redundant, redundancy Note the *an*. The plural of *redundancy* is *redundancies* ⇒ **-y.**

referral, referred, referring The final *r* of *refer* is doubled before -*al*, -*ed* and -*ing* because the stress is on *fer* ⇒ **doubling of final consonants.**

referee, reference The final *r* of *refer* is <u>not</u> doubled in these words because the stress is not on *fer* ⇒ **doubling of final consonants.**

reflection, reflexion Both correct, but the *ct* form is commoner.

refrigerator Notice that although there is a *d* in *fridge*, there is <u>no</u> *d* in *refrigerator*.

regretted, regretting, regrettable The *t* of *regret* is doubled before a consonant beginning with a vowel ⇒ **doubling of final consonants.**

reign Note the silent *g* in a king or queen's *reign*.

relevance, relevant Note the *lev* and the *an*.

relief, relieve *I* before *e* ⇒ **-ei-, -ie-.**

reminiscent Note the *min* and the *sc*.

remittance Note the double *t* (⇒ **doubling of final consonants**) and the *an*.

repetition, repetitive Pitfalls here are the *pet* and *it*. Notice that these two words act as spelling aids to each other, however: the *it* is clearly pronounced in *repet<u>it</u>ion*, and the *pet* in *rep<u>et</u>itive*.

reprieve *I* before *e* in this word ⇒ **-ei-, -ie-.**

require Note the spelling *req*.

resemble, resemblance Note the single *s*.

reservoir This word is related to *reserve*, which serves as a reminder that there is an *r* before the *v*.

resign, resigned Note the silent *g*, pronounced in *resignation*.

resistance, resistant Note the *an* ⇒ **-ance, -ence.**

responsible, responsibility Note the *ib* ⇒ **-able, -ible.**

restaurant The second syllable is often slurred in speech, but the *au* must not be omitted in writing.

retrieve *I* before *e* in this word ⇒ **-ei-, -ie-.**

reversible *-ible*, not *-able* ⇒ **-able, -ible.**

rhetoric, rhetorical Note the *h*.

rheumatism Note the *h* and the *e*.

rhinoceros Note the *h* and the *c*.

rhubarb Note the *h*.

rhyme, rhythm Note the *h* after the *r*, and also the *y*.

ridiculous Note the *i* of the first syllable; if in doubt, think of *rid̲icule* where it is clearly pronounced.

rigorous The *u* of *rigour* is dropped before the suffix *ous* ⇒ **-or, -our.**

riveting The *t* of *rivet* is not doubled before a suffix ⇒ **doubling of final consonants.**

sabotage Note the *bot*.

saccharine Note the double *c* and the *h*. The final *e* is optional when *saccharine* is used as a noun, obligatory in the adjective.

sacrilege, sacrilegious Note the *i* and the *eg*. As a memory aid, consider that this word is the opposite of *religious*, and the vowels *e* and *i* are the opposite way round too.

sapphire Note the double *p*.

satellite One *t*, two *l*'s.

satisfactory Note the *ory* ending.

scandalise, scandalous The *l* of *scandal* is not doubled before the suffixes *-ise* or *-ous* ⇒ **doubling of final consonants.** *Scandalise* may also correctly be written *-ize* ⇒ **-ise, -ize.**

scenery Note the *sc* and the ending *ery*.

sceptic, sceptical Note the *sc*. *Skeptic(al)* is correct only in American English.

sceptre Note the *sc* and the *re*.

schedule Note the *sch*.

scheme Note the *sch*.

science, scientific Note the *sc*.

scissors Note the *sc* and double *s*, and also the *or*.

scrupulous One *p* and one *l*.

scurrilous Two *r*'s, one *l*.

scythe Note the *sc*.

secondary Note the *ary* ending, often slurred in speech.

secretary Note the *ary* ending. If in doubt, think of the related adjective *secretarial*, when the *a* is clearly pronounced.

seize, seizure Exceptions to the general 'i before e' rule (⇒ **-ei-, -ie-**), so need particular care.

sensible *-ible*, not *-able*.

sentence Note the *ence*.

separable, separate, separation Note the *par*: if in doubt, remember that people that are *separated* are *apart*.

sergeant Everything between the *s* and the *t* is a potential source of error: note the *er*, *ge*, and *ant*.

series Note the *ie*.

several Note the *ver*, often slurred in speech.

shepherd A *shepherd* is of course a 'sheep-herd': do not forget the *h*.

sheriff One *r*, two *f*'s.

shield Note the *ie* ⇒ **-ei-, -ie-**.

shy Comparative adjective *shier* or *shyer*, superlative *shiest* or *shyest*; adverb *shyly* or *shily*; noun *shyness* ⇒ **-y**.

siege *I* before *e* in this word, as expected from the general rule ⇒ **-ei-, -ie-**.

33

sieve   *I* before *e* ⇒ **-ei-, -ie-**.

silhouette   Note the *h*.

similar, similarity, similarly   One *m*, one *l*.

simultaneous   Note the *eous*.

sincerely   Note the *cere*.

skilful, skilfully   One *l* of *skill* is dropped in *skilful* ⇒ **-l, -ll**.

slanderous   The *e* of *slander* is retained in *slanderous*, as the pronunciation indicates.

sly   Comparative adjective *slyer*, superlative *slyest*; adverb *slyly* or *slily*; noun *slyness* ⇒ **-y**.

smelt   Notice that one *l* of *smell* is dropped before the *t* suffix.

soldier   Note the *ie*.

solemn   Do not forget the final *n*: remember the pronunciation of *solemnize* and *solemnity*.

solicitor   Note the single *l*, and the <u>*or*</u> ending (⇒ **-er, -or, -ar**).

somersault   This word is <u>not</u> related to *summer*: note the spelling. (*Summersault* is, however, accepted by some people.)

sovereign, sovereignty   *Ei*, not *ie* (⇒ **-ei-, -ie-**), and note also the *ver* and silent *g*.

spaghetti   Note the *gh*.

species   Note the *ie*.

specifically   An adjective ending in *-ic* adds *ally* to form an adverb ⇒ **-ly**.

spectacles   Note the *ac*.

speech   The vowel in this word is <u>not</u> spelt the same way as that of *speak*. Take care.

spelt   Notice that one *l* of *spell* is dropped before the *-t* suffix.

spilt   One *l* of *spill* is dropped before the *-t* suffix.

spontaneous   Note the *eous*.

spring   Seasons are not normally written with an initial capital letter, but *spring* may be written *Spring* for the sake of clarity.

steadfast Note the *ea*; *stedfast* is an obsolete spelling, but retained for example in the motto of the Boys' Brigade.

stealth, stealthy Note the *ea*.

stereo Plural *stereos* ⇒ **-os, -oes.**

stomach Note the *o* and the *ch*.

subtle, subtlety, subtly Note the silent *b* in these words, and also the form of the adverb (⇒ **-ly**).

succeed Double *c*, as the pronunciation indicates, and note also the *ceed* ending (⇒ **-cede, -ceed, -sede**).

success, succession, successive, successor Double *c* and double *s*. Notice also the *or* ending of *successor* (⇒ **-er, -or, -ar**).

succinct Double *c*, as the pronunciation indicates.

succulent Note the double *c* and the *en*.

succumb Note the double *c* and the final *b*.

suddenness This word is formed from *sudden* plus *-ness*, therefore two *n*'s are needed.

sufferance, suffering These words are based on the verb *suffer*, therefore remember to write *fer* although the *e* is often slurred in speech. Do not double the *r* ⇒ **doubling of final consonants.**

suggest, suggestion Note the double *g*.

supercilious Note the *c*.

superintendent Take particular care to write *e* in the last syllable.

supersede Note the *sede* ending—this is the only word in English that ends in *sede* (⇒ **-cede, -ceed, -sede**).

supervise, supervisor These words may not be written with a *z* (⇒ **-ise, -ize**). Note also the *or* ending of *supervisor*.

suppose, supposing Note the double *p*.

surprise, surprised, surprising There are <u>two</u> *r*'s in these words. Note that they can never be written with *-ize* ⇒ **-ise, -ize.**

susceptible Note the *sc* and the ending *-ible* ⟹ **-able, -ible.**

symbol Note the *y.*

sympathy, sympathetic Note the *y.*

synthesis, synthesise, synthetic Note the *y. Synthesise* may also be written with a *z* ⟹ **-ise, -ize.**

syringe Note the *y* and the *i,* sometimes reversed in error.

syrup Note the *y.*

system Note the *y.*

systematically Note the *ally*: adjectives ending in *-ic* add *-ally* to form adverbs ⟹ **-ly.**

tariff One *r*, two *f*'s, like *sheriff.*

tattoo Two *t*'s in the middle of this word.

technically Note the *ally*: the *-ly* adverb ending is added to the adjective *technical.*

technique Note the final *que.*

televise This may not be written with a *z* ⟹ **-ise, -ize.**

temperamental Note the *per*, slurred in speech.

temperature Note the *per.*

tendency Note the *-ency.*

terrible, terrify, terror Remember the double *r.*

territory Note the double *r* and the *ory* ending, as indicated by the related word *territorial.*

thief *I* before *e,* as would be expected from the general rules ⟹ **-ei-, -ie-.**

thorough Watch the spelling of this word, and do not confuse it with *through.*

threshold Although many people pronounce this word [*thresh′hōld*], notice that there is in fact only one *h* in the middle, not two.

tobacco, tobacconist One *b*, two *c*'s—if in doubt, think of the slang form *baccy.*

today Generally written without a hyphen, but *to-day,* although rather old-fashioned, is not wrong.

tomato Plural *tomatoes* ⟹ **-os, -oes.**

tomorrow, tonight See comments at **today** above.

tragically An adjective ending in *ic* adds *-ally* to form an adverb ⟹ **-ly.**

tranquilliser, tranquillity Note that the *l* of *tranquil* is doubled, contrary to the general rule, before *-ise* and *-ity* ⟹ **doubling of final consonants.** *Tranquillizer* is also correct ⟹ **-ise, -ize.**

transferred, transferring, transferable The final *r* of *transfer* is doubled before the suffixes *-ed* and *-ing* because the stress is on the syllable *fer*, but note the spelling of *transferable* ⟹ **doubling of final consonants.**

transmitted, transmitter, transmitting The final *t* of *transmit* is doubled before a suffix ⟹ **doubling of final consonants.**

transparent Note the *ent* ending.

travelled, traveller, travelling Note that the *l* of *travel* is doubled before a suffix beginning with a vowel ⟹ **doubling of final consonants.**

treacherous, treachery Note the *ea*.

truly Unpredictably, the *e* of *true* is dropped before *-ly*.

Tuesday Note the *ue* spelling.

turquoise Note the *qu*.

twelfth Do not omit the *f*, often slurred in speech.

tyranny Note the *y* and the double *n*.

tyre A car's *tyre* is always spelt with a *y* in British English.

unconscious Note the *sci*.

underprivileged Watch the spelling of *privileged*.

underrate This word is formed from *under* plus *rate*, hence the double *r*.

unduly The *e* of *due* is dropped before *-ly*, in *duly* and *unduly* ⟹ **-e.**

unforgettable The *t* of *forget* is doubled before a suffix beginning with a vowel ⟹ **doubling of final consonants.**

unnatural This word is formed from *un-* plus *natural*, so two *n*'s are needed.

unnecessary This word is formed from *un-* plus *necessary*, so two *n*'s are needed.

usually This word is formed from *usual* plus *-ly*, hence the double *l*. Note also the *ua*.

vaccinate, vaccination Two *c*'s, one *n*.

vacuum One *c*, two *u*'s.

valley Plural *valleys* ⇒ **-y**.

valuable Note the *-able* ending.

vanilla One *n*, two *l*'s.

vegetable Remember the *e* of the second syllable: if in doubt, think of *vegetation*.

vehicle Remember the *h*, pronounced in the related adjective *vehicular*.

video Plural *videos* ⇒ **-os, -oes**.

vigorous The *u* of *vigour* drops before the suffix *-ous* ⇒ **-or, -our**.

villain Watch you do not write '*villian*'.

visitor Note the *or* ending ⇒ **-er, -or, -ar**.

voluntary Note the *ary* ending, often slurred in speech.

Wednesday The *d* is often slurred in speech. Remember it in writing.

weigh, weight *Ei*, not *ie* ⇒ **-ei-, -ie-**. If in doubt, remember the spelling of *eight*.

weird *Ei* in this word, contrary to what would be expected from the general rule ⇒ **-ei-, -ie-**.

whisky, whiskey Both forms are correct, depending on the origin of the drink: Scotch *whisky* but Irish or American *whiskey*; plurals respectively *whiskies* and *whiskeys* ⇒ **-y**.

wholly The *e* of *whole* is dropped, contrary to the general rule, before *-ly* is added ⇒ **-e**.

withhold   Note the double *h* in this word, as indicated by the pronunciation.

woollen, woolly   Note the double *l*'s ⇒ **doubling of final consonants.**

worshipped, worshipper, worshipping   Note the double *p*'s, contrary to what would be expected from the general rule ⇒ **doubling of final consonants.**

yield   *I* before *e*, in accordance with the general rule ⇒ **-ei-, -ie-.**

yoghurt, yoghourt   Both correct.

zigzagged, zigzagging   Note the double *g*'s, contrary to the general rule ⇒ **doubling of final consonants.**

2.
Words Liable to be Confused

The words listed in this chapter are ones which are liable to be confused or misspelt because of their similarity in sound or spelling. Each pair or set of words is distinguished by means of brief definitions and examples of use. Cross-references with an arrow (⇒) are to the entries in chapter 4, *The General Rules of English Spelling*, in which the points are treated in more detail.

accede, exceed
To **accede** to something is to agree to it: *He acceded to my request*. To **accede** to the throne is to become king or queen. To **exceed** is to go beyond or to be greater than: *He exceeded the speed limit; His success exceeded all his expectations*.

accept, except
To **accept** something is to take something offered: *He accepted their gift*. **Accept** also means 'to believe' or 'to agree to': *We accept your account of what happened; It is generally accepted that such behaviour is immoral; It was an accepted fact.*
Except means 'not including': *They're all here except John*. **Except**, as a verb, means 'to leave out, exclude': *I must except you from my criticisms.*

access, excess
Access means 'right of way, approach, entry': *We gained access to the house through a window; Students do not have access to the books on the fifth floor*. **Access** may also be used in the sense of 'a sudden attack or fit': *an access of rage.*
Excess means 'too much': *We eat well, but not to excess; an excess of alcohol; excess baggage*. It also means 'an outrageous act': *The excesses of the soldiers were condemned.*

adapter, adaptor
Both spellings are correct, but have slightly different meanings.
An **adapter** is used in the general sense of 'someone or something that adapts', as in *the adapter of a play for television.*
An **adaptor** is specifically a piece of equipment which may be attached to something else for some purpose: *an adaptor for an electrical plug.*

addition, edition
An **addition** is 'something added', or 'the act of adding': *an addition to the family; I'm not any good at addition.*
An **edition** is a number of copies of a book or newspaper printed at a time, or the form in which they are produced: *the evening edition of the newspaper; Is there a paperback edition of his book?*

advice, advise
Advice is a noun: *She gave him some good advice.* **Advise** is a verb: *She advised him to go.*
Note that **advise** must never be spelt with a *z* ⇒ **-ise, -ize.**

affect, effect
Affect is a verb meaning 'to have an influence on, cause a change in': *Your answer will not affect my decision; The accident has affected his eyesight.*
Effect can be used as both a noun and a verb. As a verb, it means 'to cause, bring about': *He tried to effect a reconciliation between his parents.* As a noun, it means 'result, consequence, impression': *He has recovered from the effects of his illness; Your action will have little effect on him.*

aid, aide
Aid means 'help': *aid to developing countries; The burglar was aided and abetted by his brother.*
An **aide** is an assistant to someone important: *The President called a meeting of his aides.*

allay, alley, ally

Allay means 'to make less': *He strove to allay their fears.*

An **alley** is a narrow street, or a place for playing certain games: *He ran through the streets and alleys*; *a bowling alley.*

An **ally** is a person, country or whatever joined to or working with another because of political agreement or friendship: *The two countries were allies at that time*; *She made an ally of the other new girl in the office.* **Ally** may also be used as a verb: *Small countries must ally themselves with larger countries in order to survive.*

allude, elude

To **allude** to something is to speak of it indirectly or to mention it in passing: *He did not allude to the previous speaker's remarks.*

To **elude** means 'to escape or avoid', as in *He eluded his pursuers*, or 'to be too difficult to understand', 'to be unable to be remembered', as in *The meaning of this poem eludes me* and *I know her face but her name eludes me.*

allusion, illusion see **illusion.**

ally, allay, alley see **allay.**

altar, alter

Altar is a noun: *the altar in a church.*

Alter is a verb: *The town has altered a lot in the last two years.*

amend, emend

These two words are frequently confused because their meanings are very similar. To **amend** something is to alter, improve, or correct it: *We shall amend the error as soon as possible*; *We wish to amend the law/constitution.*

Emend means specifically 'to correct the errors in' a book or other piece of writing: *We will emend your manuscript where necessary.*

angel, angle

An **angel** is 'a messenger or attendant of God': *The angels announced the birth of Christ.* The spelling of this word must not be confused with that of **angle**, as in *an angle of 90°*; *What is your angle on this?*

annex, annexe

Annex, stressed on the second syllable, is a verb meaning 'to add, attach, take possession of': *The USSR annexed Latvia during the Second World War.*

The noun, stressed on the first syllable, may be spelt with or without a final *e*, but the form with the *e* is commoner: *a hotel annexe*; *The school's first form is taught in the annexe.*

arc, ark

An **arc** is a curved line: *the arc of a circle*; *an arc light.* An **ark** is a type of boat: *Noah's ark.*

artist, artiste

An artist is a person who paints pictures or one who is skilled in another of the fine arts such as sculpture or music: *a stained-glass artist.* In a more general sense, **artist** may be applied to anyone who shows great skill in what he or she does: *He is a real artist with a fishing-rod.*

An **artiste** (pronounced [*är-tēst'*]) is a performer in a theatre or circus, e.g. a singer, dancer, juggler, comedian, or, rather less frequently, an actor. **Artist** may also be used in this sense.

ascent, assent

Ascent has to do with climbing or rising: *the ascent of Mount Everest*; *his ascent of the throne*; *the steep and slippery ascent to the summit.*

Assent means 'agreement' or 'to agree (to)': *The Queen gave the royal assent to the new act of Parliament*; *They assented to the proposals.*

aural, oral see **oral.**

bail, bale
Bail is money given to a court of law to gain the release of an untried prisoner until the time of his trial. To **bail out** a person is to get the person released from prison by providing bail.
To **bale out** means either 'to remove water from a boat' or 'to parachute from a plane in an emergency'. The spelling **bail out** is also possible with these meanings, but is much less common than **bale out.**

baited, bated
Note the difference in spelling between *a baited trap* and *with bated breath.*

bale, bail see **bail.**

ballet, ballot
Ballet is a type of dancing. A **ballot** is a method of voting: *They held a ballot to choose a new chairman.*

base, bass
Base means 'basis, foundation, lowest point': *The base of the statue is made of stone; This paint has an oil base; an army base.*
Bass is a musical term: *He sings bass; a double bass; a bass guitar.*

bated, baited see **baited.**

birth, berth
Birth means 'being born': *the birth of his first child.* A **berth** is a sleeping-place or mooring-place: *a berth on a ship; the ship's berth in the port.* **Berth** may also be used as a verb: *The ship has berthed in London.*

bloc, block

A **bloc** is a group of nations, etc. who have an interest or purpose in common: *the European trade bloc*; *the Communist bloc*. In all other senses the correct spelling is **block**: *a block of wood*; *a block of flats*; *a road block*; *a chopping-block*; *a fallen tree blocked his path*.

blond, blonde

Blond is masculine, **blonde** feminine: *He is blond*; *She is blonde*; *She is a blonde*; *She has blonde hair*; *He has blond hair*. Some authorities would allow *She has blond hair* since here the **blond** refers not to *she* but *hair*, but *She has blonde hair* is commoner.

born, borne

Borne is the usual past participle of the verb *to bear*, both in the senses of 'to carry' and 'to give birth to': *He was borne shoulder-high after his victory*; *She has borne him seven children*.
Born may only be used, and must be used, in passive constructions when the verb is not followed by the preposition *by*: *She was born in London*; *She was born of Indian parents*, but *She was borne by an Indian girl*.

bough, bow

The **bough** of a tree, but the **bow** of a boat. **Bow** is also the correct spelling for the bending of one's body in greeting: *He bowed to the ladies*; *He made a low bow*.

boy, buoy see **buoy**.

brake, break

Brake means 'a device for stopping or slowing a car, etc.'.
Break is used for all other meanings: *The rope might break*; *If you drop the clock, you will break it*; *I never break a promise*; *a break in the wall/conversation/weather*.

breach, breech

Breach means 'a break' or 'breaking', or as a verb, 'to break': *The soldiers streamed in through a breach in the castle wall*; *breach of promise*; *a breach of the peace*. (Note, as a spelling hint, that *break* and *breach* are both spelt *ea*.)

The **breech** of a gun is the rear part, where it is loaded. **Breeches** are trousers: *riding breeches.*

bridal, bridle

Bridal is an adjective related to the word *bride*: *a bridal gown*. A **bridle** is a horse's harness. As a verb, **bridle** also means 'to react angrily': *He bridled at her insulting comments.*

broach, brooch

To **broach** a subject is to bring it up, begin to talk about it. **Brooch** is the spelling for the decoration worn on clothing.

buoy, boy

Do not forget the *u* when referring to the **buoy** floating as a marker out at sea. **Buoy** is used as a verb, meaning 'to keep afloat', and figuratively 'to keep up': *It is cruel to buoy up his hopes if you know he is going to fail.*

cannon, canon

With two *n*'s in the middle, a **cannon** is a large gun. A **canon**, with a single *n*, is a churchman.

canvas, canvass

Canvas is a material: *a canvas tent*; *a canvas for painting on*. To **canvass** is to ask for votes or support: *We are canvassing for the Alliance.*

censor, censure

A **censor** is an official who examines books, films, letters, etc. and who has the power to delete parts of the material or to forbid publication, showing, etc. **Censure** is criticism or blame. Both words may be used as verbs: *His letters were censored*; *He was censured for staying away from work.*

choose, chose
Choose is the basic form and present tense of the verb, **chose** the past tense: *Would you like to choose a prize?*; *I always choose very carefully*; *I chose to ignore his silly remarks yesterday.*

chord, cord see **cord.**

coarse, course
Coarse is an adjective meaning 'rude, crude, rough': *coarse cloth*; *coarse behaviour.* **Course** is the correct spelling for the noun meaning 'series, route, etc.', and for the verb meaning 'to run': *We're off course*; *Of course I knew that*; *Tears coursed down her cheeks.*

collage, college
A common error is to spell **college** (= a place where people study) with an *a.* **Collage** (pronounced [*ko-läzh'*]) is the art of making pictures by pasting pieces of paper, cloth, etc. onto a surface.

comma, coma
A **comma** is a punctuation mark. A **coma** is a state of unconsciousness.

complement, compliment
A **complement** is 'that which, with some other thing, makes something which is complete or perfect', as in *Good wine is a complement to good food*; *Intuition is a complement to reason.* A ship's **complement** is the full number of officers and crew that the ship has or ought to have. A **compliment** is 'an expression of praise or flattery', as in *He is always paying me compliments.*
The same distinction applies to the verbs **complement** and **compliment** (*Good wine complements good food*; *He complimented her on her work*) and to the adjectives **complementary**

47

and **complimentary** (*These notes are complementary to the ones I gave you last week; complimentary remarks about a person's ability; a complimentary ticket*).

confident, confidant(e)

The confusion that exists between these two words is more a matter of spelling than of meaning, since the first word is an adjective, the second a noun. **Confident** means 'having a great deal of trust or assurance, having a strong belief', as *He is confident of winning; I'm confident that he will win.*
Confidant and the feminine form **confidante** mean 'someone in whom you confide, to whom you confide your secrets'.

cord, chord

Cord is the only correct spelling for the word which means 'string or cable' or 'a ribbed fabric': *They tied his hands with a piece of cord; a dress of brown cord.*
Both **cord** and **chord** may be used for the parts of the body known as the *vocal cords* and the *spinal cord*, but **cord** is nowadays the preferred form. In the musical and geometrical senses, **chord** alone is correct: *A chord is a number of notes played together; the chord of a circle.*

corps, corpse

These two words are unlikely to be confused in speech, but may be misspelt when written.
Corps (pronounced [$k\bar{o}r$]) is the word for 'a number of people working together or carrying out the same duties': *the diplomatic corps; the medical corps; an army cadet corps.* The plural of **corps** is **corps** (pronounced [$k\bar{o}rz$]).
A **corpse** (pronounced [*korps*]) is a dead body.

counsel, council

Counsel means 'advice' or 'the lawyer or lawyers acting for a person in a law-court': *counsel for the defence.* A **council** is 'a body of people who organize, control, advise, or take decisions': *a county council; the Central Council for Physical Recreation; the Privy Council.*

counsellor, councillor

A **counsellor** is a person who gives advice. A member of a council may often be correctly referred to as a **councillor**, especially if the council is one of the various bodies of people elected to control the workings of local government in counties, regions, etc.: *a local councillor.* However, if the function of a **council** is to give advice (i.e. **counsel**) its members will more correctly be referred to as **counsellors**: *the king's wise counsellors; marriage guidance counsellors; Privy Counsellors (Privy Councillors is also correct).*

course, coarse see coarse.

curb, kerb

A **curb** is something which holds back, restrains or controls: *We'll have to put a curb on his wild enthusiasm.* The word may also be used as a verb: *Curb your enthusiasm!*
A **kerb**, in British English, is the edging of a pavement. In American English, this also is spelt **curb.**

currant, current

Care must be taken with the spelling of these words. A **currant** is a fruit. A **current** is a flow of air, water or electricity. **Current** is also the correct spelling of the adjective, as in *current affairs.*

dependant, dependent

In British English, **dependant** is a noun meaning 'a person who is supported by another' and **dependent** is an adjective meaning 'depending (on)'.
In American English, both the noun and the adjective are generally spelt **dependent**. For further discussion of the *a/e* problem in similar words ⇒ **-ance, -ence.**

desert, dessert

Deserts pronounced [*dez'ərts*] are areas of hot, dry, barren country. Pronounced [*di-zûrts'*], **deserts** are what someone deserves; this word almost always occurs nowadays in the phrase *to get one's (just) deserts* 'to suffer the (usually bad) fate one deserves'. **Dessert** (pronounced [*di-zûrt'*]) is the sweet course of a meal: *We had strawberries and cream for dessert.*

device, devise

Device is a noun: *a device for boring holes.* **Devise** is a verb: *He devised a cunning plan.*

Note that **devise** may not be spelt with a *z* ⇒ **-ise, -ize.**

discrete, discreet

These words derive from the same Latin word, but in English they are different words with separate meanings: **discreet** means 'prudent, cautious, not saying or doing anything that might cause trouble', as in *My secretary won't ask awkward questions, she is very discreet*, whereas **discrete** means 'separate, not attached to others', as in *a suspension of discrete particles in a liquid.*

Note that **discretion** means 'discreetness', not 'discreteness'.

divers, diverse

Divers means 'several', **diverse** means 'various, different'.

draft, draught

In British English, a **draft** is 'a rough sketch or outline' (*a rough draft of my speech*) or 'an order to a bank for the payment of money' (*a bank draft for £40*). A **draught** is 'a current of air', 'a quantity of liquid drunk at one time' (*He took a long draught of beer*), 'the amount of water a boat requires to float' (*This boat has a shallow draught*), 'beer taken from a barrel' (*draught beer*), and 'one of the pieces used in the game of *draughts*'.

In American English, **draft** is the normal spelling for all the above meanings.

dose, doze

A **dose** is an 'amount': *a dose of medicine; a nasty dose of flu.*
As a verb it means 'to give medicine, etc. to': *She dosed him with cough-mixture.*
Doze with a *z* means 'sleep': *The old lady dozed in her armchair.*

dual, duel

Dual and **duel** are both connected with the concept of 'two'.
Dual is an adjective: *a dual carriageway.* A **duel** is a fight or contest.
As a spelling hint, remember that **dua̲l** is an *a̲djective.*

dying, dyeing

Dying is the present participle of the verb **die**, as in *He is dying of cancer;* **dyeing** is the present participle of the verb **dye,** as in *They are dyeing their shirts and socks red* (⟹ **-e**).

edition, addition see **addition.**

effect, affect see **affect.**

elicit, illicit

Elicit is a verb meaning 'to get (information etc. from someone)': *The police elicited a confession from him.*
Illicit is an adjective which means 'unlawful, not permitted': *the illicit sale of alcohol.*

eligible, illegible

These two words are sometimes confused in writing, although it takes very little thought to clear up any potential confusion.
Illegible clearly means, from the structure of the word, 'not legible': *The signature on the document is illegible.* **Eligible** means 'suitable, qualified, entitled': *She is eligible for promotion; Am I eligible for unemployment benefit?*

elude, allude see **allude.**

emend, amend see **amend.**

emigrant, immigrant see **immigrant.**

eminent, imminent
Eminent means 'outstanding, distinguished, famous', as in *an eminent lawyer.*
Imminent means 'likely to happen very soon', and is used mostly of unpleasant or undesirable things, as in *imminent danger*; *A storm is imminent.*

enquire, inquire
To most people **enquire** and **inquire**, and **enquiry** and **inquiry**, are simply alternative spellings. There are some who maintain that **enquire** and **enquiry** are to be preferred when all that is meant is a simple asking and **inquire/inquiry** when a more detailed investigation is meant, but this distinction is not recognized by many authorities on English and is not adhered to by many speakers of English, although in phrases such as *court of inquiry*, which imply a detailed investigation, **inquiry** is the form normally used, not **enquiry**.

ensure, insure see **insure.**

envelop, envelope
Envelop is a verb meaning 'to surround, cover': *She enveloped herself in a thick cloak*; *mist enveloped the hillside.*
Envelope is the correct spelling for the cover one puts a letter in.

exceed, accede see **accede.**

except, accept see **accept.**

excess, access see **access.**

exercise, exorcise
Ghosts and spooks are **exorcised**, legs and pets need **exercise**.
Exercise may not be spelt with a *z*, but **exorcise** may equally
correctly be written **exorcize** ⇒ **-ise, -ize.**

farther, further see **further.**

flair, flare
A **flair** is a natural ability or cleverness: *She has a flair for
languages.*
A **flare** is something which burns or shines: *They lit the flares
when they heard the sound of the plane.*
Flare is also the correct spelling in the sense of 'to become
wider': *The trouser legs flare slightly at the bottom.*

floe, flow
Floe is the spelling for 'a field of floating ice'. In all other senses
the spelling is **flow**.

forebear, forbear
A **forebear** is an ancestor. The word may also be spelt **forbear**.
As a verb, **forbear** means 'not to do (something)': *We must
forbear from talking about it.*

foregone, forgone
A **foregone** conclusion is an obvious or inevitable conclusion,
one which, in a sense, you already know before. To **forgo**
something is to do without it.

further, farther
Further is now commoner than **farther**. **Farther** may only be
used when there is an actual sense of 'distance' involved in the
meaning, as in *I cannot walk any farther.* **Further** may also be
used in this sense, and must be used when the sense is 'more',
'additional', 'beyond this stage', etc., as in *I would like to make
a further point; further education; closed until further notice.*

Further, and not **farther,** is also used as a verb meaning 'to help to proceed towards success, completion, etc.', as in *This will further his promotion prospects.*

gamble, gambol
Lambs **gambol,** patrons of a casino **gamble.**

gaol, goal
Gaol is jail, **goal** isn't.

gild, guild
Gild means 'to cover with gold': *Could we gild that picture-frame?* A **guild** is a society or association.

gilt, guilt
Gilt is the gold or gold-like material used for gilding. **Guilt** is shame or blame: *a feeling of guilt; We know he did it, but how do we prove his guilt?*

goal, gaol see **gaol.**

grill, grille
To **grill** is 'to cook under direct heat': *Shall I grill the chops?* It is also used of the apparatus used for grilling or the food grilled.
A **grille** is 'a framework of bars over a window or door'. This may also be spelt **grill.**

guild, gild see **gild.**

guilt, gilt see **gilt.**

hail, hale
Hail is the correct spelling for the small balls of ice that fall like rain, and for the verb meaning 'to shout, call': *The sailors hailed the passing ship.*
Note also that people **hail from** somewhere.

Hale is found in the phrase **hale and hearty**. As a spelling hint, notice that **hail**, *rain* and *sailors* have the same spelling for the vowel, and it may help also to know that **hale** and *whole* are related.

hangar, hanger
Aeroplanes are kept in **hangars**, clothes are hung up on **hangers**.

hoard, horde
A **hoard** is a store or hidden stock of something. A **horde** is a crowd or large number of people, etc.: *Hordes of tourists come here every year.*

idle, idol
Idle is an adjective meaning 'lazy, not working': *an idle boy*; *The ships were lying idle in the harbour.* It may also be used as a verb: *He is just idling the hours away.*
An **idol** is something which is worshipped as a god: *stone idols.*

illegible, eligible see **eligible.**

illicit, elicit see **elicit.**

illusion, allusion
An **illusion** is a false impression, or something which causes a false impression, which is accepted provisionally or temporarily (until further experience provides counter-evidence), or perhaps not accepted or believed at all: *She used to believe that all politicians were honest, but a series of scandals shattered her illusions; The lines he had drawn did not look parallel, but he knew that was only an optical illusion.*
An **allusion** is a passing hint at or indirect reference to (something): *Classical Chinese poetry is often difficult to understand because of the many allusions to people and things modern readers know nothing about.*

immigrant, emigrant
An **immigrant** is an 'in-migrant', i.e. a migrant into a country.
An **emigrant** is a migrant out of a country.
Similarly with **immigration** and **emigration**.

imminent, eminent see **eminent**.

inquire, enquire see **enquire**.

insure, ensure
These words are sometimes confused. To **insure** someone or
something is to arrange for the payment of a sum of money in
the event of loss, accident or injury: *He insured his life for
£20 000*. To **ensure** means 'to make sure': *You should ensure that
your television set is switched off at night.*

its, it's
Its is the possessive form of *it*: *The dog buried its bone.*
It's means 'it is' or 'it has': *It's going to rain*; *It's got to stop
raining sometime.*

kerb, curb see **curb.**

lair, layer
An animal's den or house is its **lair**. A **layer** is a thickness, covering or stratum: *a layer of icing on the cake*; *a layer of clay.*

lightning, lightening
Note that the **lightning** which often accompanies thunder has
no *e* in it, unlike the present participle of the verb **lighten.**

loathe, loath, loth
To **loathe** is 'to dislike': *I loathe rice pudding.* **Loath** (or **loth**)
means 'unwilling': *I am lo(a)th to spend much money on this
old car.*

loose, lose
Loose means 'not tight': *a loose screw.* **Lose** is a verb: *She is scared she will lose her job*; *I always lose at cards.*

madam, madame
The normal form of this word in English is **madam**, pronounced [*ma′dəm*], often written with a capital. It is used as a polite term of respect, as in *I will see if I can find the coat you are looking for, madam,* and is sometimes used before the title of a lady's official position when she is being addressed formally, as in *Madam Chairman.*
Madame, pronounced [*ma′dəm*] or [*ma-däm′*], is the French equivalent of *Mrs,* and is correctly used instead of *Mrs* when referring to ladies from French-speaking countries.

mat, matt
There is no problem with the spelling of **mat** meaning 'rug'. Note, however, that in the sense of 'dull, not glossy', the spelling is generally **matt** (although, less commonly, both **mat** and **matte** are found): *photographs with a matt finish*; *matt paint.*

meat, meet, mete
Few people make mistakes with the spelling of **meat** (= flesh) and **meet** (= to come together with, come face to face with). Note that in the old sense of 'proper, suitable', the spelling is again **meet** (*It is not meet that you should talk to one such as me*), and that one **metes out** punishment: *The judge meted out severe sentences to all the criminals.*

meter, metre
Be careful not to confuse these words: **metre** is a unit of measurement, **meter** an instrument for measuring (e.g. *a gas meter*). In American English, both words are spelt **meter.**

miner, minor
A **miner** works in a mine. **Minor** is the correct spelling for the word meaning 'lesser, less important, younger, a young person

not yet legally an adult': *a minor road*; *He had a minor part to play in the operation*; *In Britain, people under 18 are minors.*
If in doubt about the spelling of **minor**, think of *min<u>o</u>rity*, in which the *o* is clearly pronounced.

moral, morale
Moral is an adjective meaning 'relating to good character or correct behaviour': *a very moral life*. It is also the correct spelling for the **moral** of a story.
Morale is level of courage or confidence: *In spite of the defeat, the soldiers' morale was high.*

motive, motif
A **motive** is 'a reason for doing something': *The police could not establish any motive for the crime.*
A **motif** is a pattern or repeated design or a repeated feature in a play or musical work.

naught, nought see **nought**.

naval, navel
Naval is the adjective relating to the navy: *naval uniform.* **Navel** with an *e* is the small hollow in the centre of the abdomen. A **navel orange** is so called from the navel-like depression in the skin which is a feature of this particular variety of orange.

net, nett
Net is the more commonly found form of this word: *a fishing net*; *The ball hit the net*; *The net profit was £100*; *The sugar weighs one kilo net.*
In the 'profit' and 'weight' senses, **nett** is also correct.

nougat, nugget
Nougat is a kind of sticky sweet, pronounced [$n\overline{oo}'ga$] or [$nug'ət$]. This must not be confused with gold **nuggets**.

nought, naught

Nought and **naught** are in origin one and the same word, the variant spellings matching **bought** and **caught** respectively. However, in present-day English, the two spellings are normally kept separate: **nought** is a zero, the figure 0; **naught** is nothing, usually found in phrases such as *come to naught, set at naught.*

nugget, nougat see **nougat.**

o, oh

Oh is the normal form in present-day English: *Oh, what a surprise!*; *Oh, look at that big red balloon!* It is normally followed by a comma or an exclamation mark except in short exclamations like *Oh no!* or *Oh dear!* **O** is now found almost only in poetry, especially when addressing someone or expressing a wish: *O Skylark, bird of heavenly joy!*; *O for the wings of a dove!* It is never separated from the following word by a comma or exclamation mark.

oral, aural

Because of their similarity in sound, **oral** and **aural** are sometimes confused. **Oral** means 'of the mouth', 'taken in by the mouth', 'spoken as opposed to written': *oral hygiene*; *an oral contraceptive*; *an oral exam.* **Aural** means 'pertaining to the ear or listening': *an exercise in aural comprehension.*

past, passed

Passed is the past tense and part participle of the verb **pass**: *He has passed the exam*; *He passed me the salt and pepper.* **Past** is the form to use in all other senses: *There's no use dwelling on the past*; *past participle*; *past mistakes*; *The time for doing that is long past.*

pastel, pastille

A **pastille** is a type of sweet. **Pastels** are artists' crayons, or pictures drawn with them, hence also **pastel** colours.

pedal, peddle
You **pedal** a bicycle, but note that a **pedlar peddles** goods from door to door.

personnel, personal
Personnel is a noun meaning 'the people employed in a shop, factory, company, etc.': *Our personnel are very highly trained.* Do not confuse **personnel** (with two *n*'s and an *e*) with the adjective **personal** (one *n* and an *a*): *That is my personal opinion*; *He made a personal appearance*; *personal freshness.*

plane, plain
Plane is the correct spelling for an aeroplane or certain parts of one (*the tail plane*), a type of tree, a tool for smoothing wood, a level or standard (*Man is on a higher plane than the apes*), a level surface in geometry, and, in a verbal sense, to glide smoothly.
Plain means 'clear', 'honest', 'not pretty' etc. A **plain** is a large flat stretch of land.
A straightforward easy task may be said to be **plain** sailing.

practice, practise
Practice is the noun, **practise** the verb.

pray, prey see **prey.**

precede, proceed see **proceed.**

prey, pray
Prey is that which a bird or animal hunts and kills for food: *The lion carried off its prey.* **Prey** can also be used as a verb: *Hawks prey on smaller birds*; *Fears preyed on her mind*. To **pray** is to say a prayer: *She prayed to God to help her.*

principal, principle

These two words are one of the most frequently confused and misspelt pair of words in English. As an adjective, **principal** means 'most important': *Shipbuilding is one of Britain's principal industries.* As a noun **principal** means 'the head of a school, college or university' or 'the leading actor, singer or dancer in a theatrical production'.

The word **principle** can only be used as a noun. It means 'a general rule' or 'the theory underlying a method or way of working': *the principles of economic theory; the principle of the jet engine; I agree with the idea in principle; He refused to do it on principle; It is against my principles to borrow money.*

prise, prize

One **prises** open a box with a knife, but one **prizes** a person's friendship. **Prizes** are also what are awarded for good work or won in games and competitions.

proceed, precede

Proceed and **precede** are often confused, and where not confused, misspelt.

Note the spelling of the second syllable of each of these words. (For further comments ⇒ **-cede, -ceed, -sede**).

To **proceed** is 'to continue, to go on, to begin to do something or follow a course of action': *They proceeded with their work; They proceeded to ask a lot of stupid questions.* To **precede** is 'to go before': *She preceded him into the room; He is mentioned in this chapter and also in the preceding one.*

prophecy, prophesy

Prophecy is the noun, **prophesy** the verb.

quiet, quite

No-one really confuses these words, but slips of the pen are common. Take care!

raise, raze see **raze**.

rapped, rapt, wrapped
Rapped and **wrapped** pose few problem: *He rapped on the door with his stick*; *He wrapped up the presents*. But note the spelling of **rapt** (= fascinated, attentive), as in *He listened to the speaker with rapt attention*.

raze, raise
To **raze** is 'to destroy completely': *The houses were razed to the ground in the fire*. The spelling **rase** is also correct, but less common. These words must not be confused with **raise** meaning 'to lift up, increase'.

reign, rein
A king **reigns**, a horse has **reins**.

review, revue
A **revue** is a type of amusing theatre show. A **review** is a report, study or critical consideration of something: *Have you seen the review of his latest novel in today's paper?*; *We'll have a review of her progress at the end of the month*.

rhyme, rime
A **rhyme** is a short poem. In this sense, **rime** is archaic, and only found in certain poems, such as Coleridge's *The Rime of the Ancient Mariner*.
Rime is 'thick, white frost'.

roll, rôle
Rôle, or **role** (without the accent), is 'a person's part in a play' or 'function in some activity': *He is playing a very demanding rôle—he has to pretend to be mad*; *The police asked the boy what his rôle had been in the robbery*.
Other meanings are spelt **roll**: *a roll of paper*; *bread and rolls*; *The ball rolled under the table*.

sceptic, septic

A **sceptic** is a person who believes that nothing can be known with absolute certainty, or, more loosely, a person who is unwilling to believe some particular statement, theory, etc.: *Most people now accept this hypothesis, but there are still a few sceptics.* **Septic** means 'full of, or caused by, germs that are poisoning the blood': *a septic finger/wound; septic poisoning.*

stanch, staunch

Stanch and **staunch** are both correct in the sense of 'stopping a flow of blood'. **Staunch** alone is correct in the sense of 'firm, trusty, steadfast': *a staunch supporter of the party.*

stationary, stationery

Stationary is an adjective, meaning 'not moving': *a stationary vehicle.* **Stationery** is a noun meaning 'paper, envelopes, etc.': *This firm spends far too much money on stationery.*

As an aid to spelling, remember that pa_rked ca_rs are **stationa_ry**, pap_er for lett_ers is **statione_ry**.

staunch, stanch see **stanch**.

stile, style see **style**.

storey, story

Both **storey** and **story** may correctly be used for 'the floor or level in a building', but **storey** is by far the commoner: *an apartment block of seventeen storeys.*

Story alone is correct for 'a tale, account of events'.

straight, strait

These words are sometimes confused. **Straight** is generally used as an adjective: *a straight line; Your tie isn't straight; It was so funny I could hardly keep my face straight when I was telling him; I can never get a straight answer from him.* **Straight** may also be used as an adverb meaning 'in a straight line, not bending, curving or wandering' and as a noun meaning 'the straight part of something': *Go straight home*; *He walked straight across the garden*; *The horses are in the final straight* (= the straight part of a racecourse). **Straight** is also used in compounds and phrases such as *straightforward*, *straight away*, and *the straight and narrow*.

Strait is an old adjective meaning 'narrow', 'confined' or 'confining'. It is now found only in compound words such as *strait-jacket* and *strait-laced*. As a noun, **strait** is still in common use, especially in the plural. It means 'a narrow strip of sea between two pieces of land' as in *the Straits of Gibraltar* and *the Bering Strait*, or 'difficulty, need' as in *She had been in great straits financially since her husband died* and *in dire straits*.

The above distinction applies to **straightened** and **straitened**; *The dentist straightened her teeth*; *She is living in straitened circumstances*.

sty, stye

Pigs live in a **sty**. A **stye**, or **sty**, is a swelling on the eyelid.

style, stile

A **stile** is a step or set of steps for climbing over a wall or fence. **Style** is elegance, or one's manner of doing things.

swat, swot

Swat means 'to hit' and is applied especially to the hitting of flies, wasps and other insects: *He swatted the fly with a folded newspaper*. **Swot** is a colloquial term for 'to study': *She stayed in her room and swotted for her exam*.

their, there, they're

They're is short for 'they are', so there should be no difficulty in spelling it correctly. **Their** means 'of them': *Where should they put their shoes?* In other senses, **there** is the correct spelling: *Put it down over there*; *There has been an accident*; *There he goes now*.

Theirs and **there's** are sometimes also confused. **Theirs** means 'of them': *We can put ours here and they can put theirs over there.* **There's** is short for 'there is' or 'there has': *There's something interesting going on over there; There's been an accident.*

tire, tyre
To **tire** is 'to become, or cause to become, weary': *Don't tire yourself out.* The normal spelling for the thick rubber strip or tube around a wheel is **tyre** in British English, but **tire** in American English.

troop, troupe
Troop denotes a group of soldiers, certain animals or ordinary people: *a scout troop; a troop of monkeys.* **Troupe** is used of performers: *a troupe of acrobats.*

tyre, tire see tire.

waive, wave
To **waive** is to 'give up, abandon': *He waived his claim to the land.* All other senses are spelt **wave**: *the waves on the sea; He waved good-bye; a crime wave.*

who's, whose
Who's is short for 'who is' or 'who has': *Who's coming today?; Who's got my pencil?*
Whose means 'of whom': *Whose book is this?*

wrapped, rapped, rapt see rapped.

you're, your
You're is short for 'you are': *You're a fool.*
Your means 'of you': *Your book is over there.*

3.
One Word or Two?

In this chapter, you will find notes on phrases which are incorrectly written as single words, words which are split up and written as if they were phrases, and words and phrases which are similar in sound and which are therefore confused with one another.

all right, alright
Although appearing with increasing frequency in present-day English, **alright** is not yet a generally accepted spelling of **all right**. At present the only correct form is **all right**.

already, all ready
Already is an adverb expressing certain notions of time: *Are you leaving already?*; *He had already left when I arrived.*
All ready is a phrase in which the words **all** and **ready** carry their own separate meanings: *Are you all ready now?*

altogether, all together
Altogether means 'completely', 'in total', or 'all things considered' as in *I'm not altogether satisfied with your work*; *Altogether, we've collected £500*; *I'm wet, I'm tired and I'm cold. In fact, altogether I'm feeling pretty miserable* respectively.
All together means 'all in a group in one place', as in *I'll put these books all together on the shelf.*
All together can be separated by other words, as in *I'll put all these books together on the shelf*; **altogether** is a single word and can never be split.

anyone, any one
Anyone means 'any person at all': *Anyone could tell you the answer to that*; *Is there anyone there?*

Any one means 'any single one' and can be applied to persons or things: *Look at the cards in my hand and choose any one of them.*

Notice, as a spelling hint, that **anyone** can be replaced by **anybody,** whereas **any one** cannot be: *Is there anybody there?*

can not, cannot

In British English, the form **cannot** must be used unless the word **not** is linked to the following word or words in a way that requires it to have particular emphasis. Compare for example *He cannot sing* and *You cannot just walk into the room without knocking on the door first* with *He can not only sing but he dances as well.*

In American English, **can not** may be used, and is generally preferred, where British English requires **cannot.**

ever, -ever

When **ever** is used to emphasize words like *why, how, where,* etc., it is written as a separate word: *What ever shall we do?*; *How ever did you manage that?* When **ever** means 'any—at all', it is joined to the word it modifies as a suffix: *You may do whatever you please*; *Go wherever he tells you to go.*

Notice that **where ever, why ever,** etc. are questions, **wherever, whatever,** etc. parts of statements or commands.

See also **forever** below.

everyone, every one

Every one means 'each individual one', and can apply to people or things: *I examined all the cups, and found that every one had a flaw in it.* **Everyone** means 'every person, all people (thought of as a group rather than as individuals)': *Everyone thinks I'm crazy*; *Everyone in this street owns a car.* **Everyone** may be replaced by **everybody**: *Everybody thinks I'm crazy.*

forever, for ever

In British English, **for ever** is more often written as two words than one, but **forever** is also correct. Some people make a distinction between **forever** meaning 'continually' and **for ever** meaning 'for all time' but, while such a distinction has much to recommend it, it is not recognized by most dictionaries or speakers of English.

In American English, **forever** is the standard form.

full, -ful

The suffix **-ful** may be added to a word denoting a container of some sort in order to form a word which denotes the amount held by such a container: *bagful, cupful, pocketful, spoonful.* It must be stressed that such words denote a quantity that could or would be held in the container, and do not imply that the substance or material is actually in the container at the time of speaking: a **cupful** of flour is still a cupful once it has been mixed with other ingredients in a bowl; a **teaspoonful** of sugar is still a teaspoonful when it has been stirred into a cup of tea or spilt on the floor.

On the other hand, phrases such as *three bags full of sand* and *five glasses full of milk* are referring to the containers (*bags, glasses*, etc.) rather than to quantities. In such constructions, **full** is an adjective describing the container, not a suffix denoting a quantity.

If the distinction between quantities and containers is kept in mind, you should have no spelling problems with words in this category.

Note   The plural of *bagful, cupful* etc. is *bagfuls, cupfuls* etc.

inasmuch as, in as much as

Both are correct, but the first form is the commoner: *It would not be completely true to say that he has retired from the company, inasmuch as he still does a certain amount of work for us.*

in fact

Always written as two words.

insofar as, in so far as
Both correct, but the second form is now the commoner: *I gave him the details in so far as I knew them.*

in spite of
Must be written as three words.

instead of
Two words.

into, in to
Into is a preposition indicating movement from outside something to a position on the inside (as in *He walked into the room*), movement against something (as in *The car ran into a lamp-post*), or a change of state or condition (as in *The wizard turned them into frogs*).
In to consists of an adverb **in** and a preposition **to**, and must not be confused with **into**. Distinguish, for example, between *He came into the room*, *He came in to tell us what had happened* and *He escorted her in to dinner* (i.e. into the room in order to have dinner, not actually into the dinner itself).

maybe, may be
Maybe means 'perhaps': *Maybe he'll come this afternoon.* **May be** is a phrase comprising the verb **may** and the verb **be**: *He may be coming this afternoon.*

no-one, no one
The same distinction may be drawn between **no-one** and **no one** as has been drawn between **anyone** and **any one**, **everyone** and **every one**: **no-one** means 'no person' and can be replaced by **nobody**, **no one** means 'no single individual (person or thing)': *Is anyone there? No, there's no-one there*; *There's nobody there*; *No one person could possibly eat all that.*
Spelling Note   Unfortunately, **no-one** is not generally used nowadays, and the non-hyphenated form **no one** is commonly

69

found where 'nobody' is meant. Both forms are quite correct, however, and where there is any possibility of ambiguity or uncertainty, the hyphenated form should certainly be used. Indeed, we would recommend that the hyphenated form be used in all cases where 'nobody' is meant, in order to preserve the parallelism of

anyone	*any one*
everyone	*every one*
no-one	*no one*

on to, onto

Unlike **into**, **onto** is not a word-form accepted by everyone. Many people still prefer **on to** as two words even in senses corresponding to **into**. However, both **on to** and **onto** must be considered correct prepositional forms in present-day English: *The book fell on to* (or *onto*) *the table*. Of course, when **on to** consists of an adverb and a preposition, it must never be written as a single word: *He went on to tell me about his life in Africa*, <u>not</u> *He went onto tell me*.

sometime, some time

Sometime means 'at some point in time': *I haven't enough time to finish this now, but I'll do it sometime*.
Some time means 'a little time': *I'll need some time to finish this*.

thank you

Should generally be written as two words, as in *Thank you for the book*, but may be hyphenated in a construction like *I would just like to say thank-you to you for the book*.

4.
The General Rules of English Spelling

abbreviations

Abbreviations are shortened forms of words, titles, phrases, etc. The main rules that you need to know about writing abbreviations are the following:

1. Abbreviations which include the final letter of the abbreviated word are nowadays usually written without full stops: *Mr, Dr, 1st, 2nd, 3rd, 4th, 4to* (= quarto), *hr* (= hour).

2. Abbreviations of the names of countries and organizations, such as *USA, USSR, UN, EEC*, are usually written without full stops, and almost always so when they are pronounced as if they were single words rather than strings of letters: *NATO, UNICEF, UNESCO, NALGO*. Sometimes this latter type of abbreviation is written as if it was a single word, with only a capital letter for the first letter: *NATO* or *Nato, UNESCO* or *Unesco*.

3. Abbreviations of metric measurements and the symbols for chemical elements are written without full stops: *km, cm, kg; C* (= carbon), *Mg* (= magnesium).

4. Other abbreviations are normally written with full stops, *ibid.* or *viz.* for example, but there is an increasing tendency to omit the full stops in these also: *e.g.* or *eg, i.e.* or *ie, B.Sc.* or *BSc, M.B.E.* or *MBE, D.F.C.* or *DFC.*

abbreviations of plural words

Abbreviations of metric measurements do not add an *s* in the plural: *3 cm* (= 3 centimetres), *50 kg* (= 50 kilograms). With many non-metric measurements, forms with or without an *s* are equally acceptable: *3 lb* or *3 lbs* (= 3 pounds), *6 oz* or *6 ozs* (= 6 ounces), but in modern practice the *s* tends to be omitted. Certain abbreviations such as *cwt* (= hundredweight), *min.* (= minute) and *sec.* (= second) never take an *s* in the plural.

-able, -ible

This pair of suffixes (or 'word-endings') give many people a great deal of trouble. The problems have their roots in Latin grammar, by the rules of which certain words would predictably end in *-abilis* and others equally predictably in *-ibilis*. Unfortunately, these rules do not apply to the grammar of English, and the choice between **-able** and **-ible** is very much less predictable. However, there are a number of hints and clues you can memorize which may help you to decide whether a particular word should be spelt with an *a* or an *i*:

1. There are many more **-able** words than **-ible** words. While this may be of little help if you want to be certain about the spelling of a particular word, it can be useful to keep in mind if you are unable to think of any other rule to apply and have to rely on guesswork: when in doubt and forced to guess, opt for **-able**.

2. If the word you want to spell is connected with words which end in *-acity*, *-ality*, *-ate*, or *-ation*, then **-able** will be the correct spelling:

adaptation	: *adaptable*	*application*	: *applicable*
capacity	: *capable*	*estimate*	: *inestimable*
hospitality	: *hospitable*	*inflammation*	: *inflammable*
separate	: *inseparable*	*transportation*	: *portable*
tolerate	: *tolerable*	*habitation*	: *uninhabitable*

3. If the ending is preceded by a hard *c*, pronounced [*k*], or a hard *g*, pronounced [*g*], the ending must be **-able** (because if it was **-ible**, the *i* would 'soften' the *c* and *g* and they would be pronounced [*s*] and [*j*]):

amicable	*implacable*	*navigable*
despicable	*irrevocable*	

4. If the part of the word that precedes the ending (the 'core' of the word, as it were) is a complete English word in itself, then the correct spelling of the ending is usually **-able**:

accept	: *acceptable*	*break*	: *breakable*
detest	: *detestable*	*fashion*	: *fashionable*
lament	: *lamentable*	*pay*	: *payable*

Exceptions There are exceptions to this rule, and unfortunately even exceptions to the exceptions. However, matters are not as bad as they might at first seem, as even the exceptions can for the most part be covered by rules:

i) If the core word is one to which *-ion* could be added to form a related word (note, not *-ation* or *-ition*, just *-ion*), then **-ible** will almost always be the correct suffix:

corrupt	: *corruption*	: *corruptible*
exhaust	: *exhaustion*	: *inexhaustible*
perfect	: *perfection*	: *perfectible*

A few words do not follow this rule:

collect : *collection*, but *collectable* or *collectible*
correct : *correction*, but *correctable* or *correctible*
detect : *detection*, but *detectable* or *detectible*
and
predict : *prediction*, but *predictable* alone correct

ii) A number of other words are exceptions to rule (4), having **-ible** where **-able** might be expected:

collapsible	*deducible*	*gullible*	*reducible*
contemptible	*discernible*	*indestructible*	*responsible*
convertible	*flexible*	*inflexible*	*sensible*
convincible	*forcible*	*irresistible*	

5. If what precedes the ending is not a recognizable English word, the ending is likely to be **-ible**. There is, for example, no word *aud* in English, therefore *audible* is correct, not *audable*. Similarly we have *credible, edible, horrible, terrible, visible,* but not *cred, ed, horr, terr,* or *vis.*

Exceptions Again there are exceptions. A number of words that one would expect by the above rule to end in **-ible** in fact end in **-able**:

affable	*equitable*	*inexorable*	*palpable*
amenable	*formidable*	*inscrutable*	*probable*
arable	*indomitable*	*malleable*	*unconscionable*
culpable	*inevitable*	*memorable*	*vulnerable*

final *e*

If the 'core' word ends in a single *e*, this *e* is normally dropped before **-able** or **-ible** is added:

advise	:	*advisable*	*complete* :	*completable*
debate	:	*debatable*	*excise* :	*excisable*
observe	:	*observable*	*use* :	*usable*

Exceptions There are exceptions to the above rule:

1. If the core word ends in 2 *e*'s, both are retained before **-able**:

agree	:	*agreeable*	*foresee* :	*foreseeable*

2. If the core word ends in *-ce* or *-ge*, the *e* is retained in order to preserve the soft [*s*] and [*j*] sounds of the *c* and *g*:

changeable	*knowledgeable*	*noticeable*
peaceable	*pronounceable*	*unchallengeable*

A small number of other words, mostly based on one-syllable 'core' words, retain, or may retain, the *e* of the core word:

blame	:	*blameable* (sometimes *blamable*)
like	:	*likeable* (sometimes *likable*)
live	:	*livable* (sometimes *liveable*)
love	:	*lovable* (sometimes *loveable*)
move	:	*movable* (sometimes *moveable*)
rate	:	*rateable* (sometimes *ratable*)
shape	:	*shapable* (sometimes *shapeable*)
size	:	*sizeable* (sometimes *sizable*)

final _y_

A final _y_ becomes _i_ before **-able**:

  classify :   _classifiable_   _rely_   :   _reliable_
  envy   :   _enviable_   _vary_   :   _variable_

(There are, in fact, no words that end in _-iible_. If the letter before the suffix is an _i_, whether or not it replaces a _y_, the ending will be **-able**:

amiable   _insatiable_   _viable_)
appreciable   _sociable_

doubled consonants

In the case of verbs whose final consonant is doubled in the formation of the present participle, the final consonant is similarly doubled in forming **-able** adjectives:

  bid   :   _bidding_   :   _biddable_
  forget :   _forgetting_   :   _unforgettable_
  stop   :   _stopping_   :   _unstoppable_

(For further details ⇒ **doubling of final consonants**.)

Exceptions Exceptions to this rule are verbs ending in _-fer_, which do not double the final _r_ before **-able**:

  prefer   :   _preferring_   :   _preferable_
  transfer :   _transferring_   :   _transferable_

-ability, -ibility, -ably, -ibly

Nouns formed from adjectives ending in **-able** and **-ible** end in **-ability** and **-ibility** respectively:

  adaptable : _adaptability_   _eligible_ : _eligibility_

Adverbs formed from adjectives ending in **-able** and **-ible** end in **-ably** and **-ibly** respectively:

  presumable : _presumably_   _responsible_ : _responsibly_

-acy, -asy

Words ending in **-acy** and **-asy** are often misspelt, _s_ being written where _c_ is correct and vice versa.

-acy

The ending **-acy** is the commoner of the two. Among words ending in **-acy** are:

accuracy	*conspiracy*	*inaccuracy*	*pharmacy*
autocracy	*delicacy*	*intimacy*	*privacy*
bureaucracy	*democracy*	*intricacy*	*supremacy*
celibacy	*diplomacy*	*meritocracy*	*theocracy*
confederacy	*fallacy*	*obstinacy*	

Spelling hints   Note that the words ending in **-cracy** are related to words ending in **-crat**, such as *aristocrat* and *bureaucrat*, and that many of the other words ending in **-acy** are related to words which end in **-ate**, e.g. *accurate, celibate, delicate, private*. This provides a useful rule of thumb which helps with at least some of the spelling problems.

-asy

There are few words which end in **-asy**. The commonest ones are

  apostasy   *ecstasy*   *fantasy*   *idiosyncrasy*

Warning   Note the correct spelling of *hypocrisy*, which has no *a* in it at all. If in doubt, think of the related words *hypocrite* and *hypocritical*.

adjectives

For the formation of adjectives ending in *-ed, -d* ⇒ **-ed, -d.**
For the formation of comparative and superlative forms ⇒ **-er, -est.**

adverbs

For the construction of adverbs ⇒ **-ly.**

-ae-, -e-

There are a number of words in English—*mediaeval, encyclopaedia, haemoglobin, aesthetic*, for example—in which the *a* is optional. In American English, the forms without the *a*—*medieval, encyclopedia*, etc.—are standard; in British English, the *a* is generally retained, except in *medieval*, which is now more common than *mediaeval*.

-ance, -ence

The choice of *a* or *e* in the ending of words such as *abundance*, *conference*, *defiance* and *intelligence* is one which causes many problems and there are, unfortunately, few easy-to-learn general rules to assist you to make the correct choice. There are, however, a number of hints and clues as to the correct spelling, and the most useful of these are given here:

1. If the letter before the ending is a 'hard' *c* or a 'hard' *g* i.e. pronounced [*k*] and [*g*] respectively, then **-ance** will be the correct spelling:

arrogance   *elegance*   *significance*

If the letter is a 'soft' *c* or *g* (i.e. pronounced [*s*] or [*j*]), the ending will almost always be **-ence** (notice that many of the words in this category have *isc* or *esc* in the syllable before the ending):

adolescence   *intelligence*   *reminiscence*
effervescence   *negligence*   *reticence*
innocence

Exceptions   Note the spelling of *allegiance* and *vengeance*.

2. Words which are related to verbs ending in *-ate* or nouns ending in *-ation* will normally end in **-ance**:

dominate : *dominance*   *tolerate* : *tolerance*
Exception   *violate* : *violence*
Other words may equally give a clue to the spelling:
ignoramus : *ignorance*   *vigilante* : *vigilance*

3. Nouns formed from verbs ending in *-ear*, *-ure*, and *-y* end in **-ance**:

ally : *alliance*   *assure* : *assurance*
appear : *appearance*   *insure* : *insurance*
Spelling note   Notice that the *y* changes to *i* before the ending, and that the final silent *e* is dropped. (For further notes on these points ⇒ **-y** and **-e**.)

4. A noun formed from a verb ending in *-ere* will end in **-ence:**

cohere : *coherence*   *revere* : *reverence*
interfere : *interference*

Exception Note the spelling of *perseverance*, an exception to rule (4).

5. *-cid-*, *-fid-*, *-sid-*, *-vid-*, *-flu-*, *-qu-* and *-sist-* are generally followed by **-ence:**

confidence   *influence*   *sequence*
eloquence   *providence*   *subsistence*

Exceptions Notice the spelling of *assistance* and *resistance*, two exceptions to the rule.

6. With verbs ending in a single vowel followed by *r*, if the vowel before the *r* is stressed, the ending for the noun will be **-ence**; if the stress is elsewhere, the ending will be **-ance.**

This is an apparently rather complicated rule, but it is in fact straightforward enough once one has grasped the principles involved, and once learned it will allow you to spell words like *occurrence*, *preference* and *utterance* correctly:

If the vowel before the *r* is stressed (that is, is louder or has more emphasis than the other vowels of the word), then the noun ending will be **-ence:**

confer' : *conference*   *deter'* : *deterrence*
occur' : *occurrence*   *prefer'* : *preference*
transfer' : *transference*

If the stress is <u>not</u> on the vowel before the *r*, the ending will be **-ance:**

hin'der : *hindrance*   *ut'ter* : *utterance*

Exception In spite of the stress pattern of the verb *dif'fer*, notice that the noun *difference* ends in **-ence.**

Spelling notes The following points should be noted:

i) You may have noticed that in some of the **-ence** category words above, the final *r* of the verb is doubled, while in other cases, it remains single. This doubling or non-doubling of the *r* depends on the stress pattern of the <u>noun</u> (not the verb): If the noun is stressed on the vowel before the *r*, double the *r*; if it isn't, don't.

This rule allows us to distinguish between the spelling of *con'ference*, *dif'ference* and *pref'erence* with the stress on the first syllable and therefore only a single *r*, and *deter'rence* and *occur'rence* with stress on the vowel before the *r* and therefore a double *r*.

ii) In a few words, the *e* before the *r* is dropped: note the spelling of *hindrance* (from *hinder*) and *remembrance* (from *remember*).

The rules given above cover many, but by no means all of the words ending in **-ance** and **-ence**. For words not covered by these guidelines, one is simply obliged to learn the correct ending by heart. If in doubt, consult a dictionary.

final *e*
The final *e* of a verb is dropped before **-ance/-ence**:

assure	:	assurance	guide	:	guidance
cohere	:	coherence	persevere	:	perseverance

doubling of final consonants
The doubling of a final *r* of a verb has been dealt with under rule (6) above. In general, with other consonants, it is safe to follow the spelling of the present participle (the *-ing* form) of the verb, i.e. when a verb doubles its final consonant in the formation of the present participle, the final consonant is doubled in the formation of an **-ance/-ence** noun:

admit	:	admitting	:	admittance
rid	:	ridding	:	riddance
excel	:	excelling	:	excellence

For further details ⇒ **doubling of final consonants.**

-ant, -ent, -ancy, -ency

Although the rules have been explained with regard to words ending in **-ance** and **-ence**, they apply equally to related words which end in **-ant/-ent** or **-ancy/-ency**. There are, however, a small group of **-ant/-ent** words which present a particular problem, in that their spelling varies according to whether the words are nouns or adjectives:

   dependant, descendant, pendant and *propellant* are nouns;
   dependent, descendent, pendent and *propellent* are adjectives.

Memory aid   If in doubt, remember that just as the indefinite article *a* is used with nouns (*a book, a dog,* etc.), so also the vowel *a* is the correct one to use for the nouns in the above list.

Warning   *Independent* is the only correct spelling, for the noun as well as the adjective.

ante-, anti-

The similarity in spelling and pronunciation between these two prefixes may lead to their being confused with each other, but if you keep their meanings in mind, there should be no reason for doubt, or confusion:

ante- means 'before', as in *antenatal* 'before birth', and *ante-room* 'a room opening into another, more important, room';

anti- means 'against' or 'opposite', as in *anti-aircraft gun*, *antibiotic* 'a medicine used against bacteria', *anticlockwise*, etc.

Spelling note   Words beginning with **ante-** should not be hyphenated. Words which begin with **anti-** are also generally written without hyphens, unless the letter following **anti-** is an *i* or a capital letter. The following words are, however, usually hyphenated:

anti-aircraft	*anti-hero*	*anti-novel*
anti-establishment	*anti-marketeer*	*anti-personnel*
anti-gravity		

apostrophe

deletions

An apostrophe is often used to show that one or more letters or figures have been omitted from a word or number: *can't* is an abbreviation of *cannot, it's* of *it is, she'll* of *she will, I'd* of *I had* or *I would, the '30s* of *the 1930s.*

Spelling note   Some words which are in origin abbreviations of longer words are now no longer written with apostrophes:

  bus   flu   phone   plane

possessives

A further use of the apostrophe is seen in the formation of possessive nouns. The general rules which apply to the use of apostrophes with possessives are quite straightforward, but there are a few important exceptions to these rules which also must be noted.

The basic rules are as follows:

The possessive form of a noun is shown, in writing, by the addition of *'s*: *the child's dog; the children's dog; James's dog; Robert Burns's dog.*

If the noun is plural and already ends in *s*, the apostrophe alone is used: *the boys' dog*, not *the boys's dog*. This applies also to certain expressions of time in which the time expression is treated as a possessive: *He's coming in two weeks' time.*

Spelling hint   Notice that in all these cases, the written form of the words mirrors the spoken form: where an additional *s* is pronounced in a spoken possessive form, it is added in the written form; where no *s* is added in pronunciation, the apostrophe alone is added in the written form.

Warning   In a few exceptional cases, a singular noun ending in *s* is followed by an apostrophe alone rather than by *'s*. The main exceptions are names whose pronunciation with an additional *s* would be difficult or clumsy: *If you compare these two cars, you'll find that the Mercedes' engine is the more powerful.* Biblical and ancient Greek and Roman names which end in *s* can also be treated in this way, as in *Moses' laws, Xerxes' army*, but although still correct, this practice is not as prevalent as it used to be. The existence of such exceptions to the general rule will not give rise to any confusion or uncertainty if it is remembered that in such cases also, the correct written form of the words reflects the pronunciation of the spoken form. In other words, if you pronounce the possessive *'s*, write it; if you don't pronounce an *s*, don't write one.

sake
It should be noted that in certain expressions with **sake**, nouns ending in an *s* sound which by the nature of the construction ought to be spelt with an *'s* are now usually written without even an apostrophe: compare *for heaven's sake* and *for goodness sake*.

pronouns
Do not use an apostrophe with possessive pronouns: the correct forms are *yours, hers, its* (*it's = it is*), *ours, theirs*. *One's*, however, is correct: *One must look after one's own family.*

Note also the possessive form *whose*, not *who's* (*who's = who is*): *Whose book is this?*

plurals
Apostrophes should *not* normally be used in the formation of plural nouns: plural forms such as *book's, bag's, lolly's* are increasingly common, and care should be taken to avoid them. An apostrophe is, however, permitted in plurals in a few specific cases, mainly for the sake of clarity:

1. An apostrophe is frequently written in the plurals of a number of short words:
do (as in *do's and don'ts*)
me (as *I feel there are two me's at the moment*)
set-to (as *I've had a few set-to's with him*)
he and *she* (as in *Are the puppies he's or she's?*)
Dos, set-tos, hes and *shes* are, however, equally correct (*mes* seems less acceptable than *hes* and *shes*, for no obvious reason).

2. When the word in the plural is the title of a book, play, etc., *'s* is often used instead of *s* alone:

There have been three <u>Macbeth's</u> (= three different versions of the play 'Macbeth') *performed in Edinburgh in the past six months.*

Here again, *s* alone is equally permissible.

3. *'s*, rather than *s*, is normal for the plural form of a word which is being quoted from something else:

There are too many <u>that's</u> in that sentence.

4. *'s* should be used to form the plural of single letters and figures:

Dot your i's and cross your t's
Write a row of 2's, then a row of 3's.

With longer numbers, e.g. in dates, both *'s* and *s* are permissible:

Were you around in the 1930's/1930s?
How many 30's/30s are there in 240?

An *s* alone should be used to form the plural of abbreviations made up of a sequence of initial letters: the correct plural of *M.P.*, for example, is *M.P.s*, not *M.P.'s*.

-ar, -er, -or see -er, -or, -ar.

-asy, -acy see -acy, -asy.

-ary, -ery, -ory

Many mistakes in spelling are made in words which end in **-ary**, **-ery** and **-ory** (such as *necessary, cemetery, factory*). Many people have great difficulty in deciding, or remembering, which words should be spelt with an *a*, which with an *e*, and which with *o*. Unfortunately, there are only a few very general hints that can be given as guidelines to the correct spelling of these words, but the following points may be of help:

1. If in doubt, look for a related word in which the vowel is more obvious. With the changing stress patterns within 'families' of words in English, it is sometimes possible to

find a related word in which the *a*, *e* or *o* is stressed and therefore more readily identifiable:

contemporaneous	:	*contemporary*
imagination	:	*imaginary*
historic	:	*history*
militate	:	*military*
secretarial	:	*secretary*

Even without a change in stress pattern, the vowels of related words may give a useful clue to the spelling of [əri] words. For example, words ending in **-ery** are often related to verbs or 'doer' nouns ending in **-er**:

baker	:	*bakery*	*brewer*	:	*brewery*
confectioner	:	*confectionery*	*distiller*	:	*distillery*
milliner	:	*millinery*	*stationer*	:	*stationery*
deliver	:	*delivery*	*upholster*	:	*upholstery*

The same parallels sometimes hold true for **-ory** and **-ary** endings:

director	:	*directory*	*predator*	:	*predatory*
burglar	:	*burglary*			

2. Words ending in **-ery** are almost all nouns. If the word you want to spell is not a noun, you can be almost certain that it will not end in **-ery**. Compare, for example, the noun *stationery* (= writing-paper, envelopes, etc.) and the adjective *stationary* (= not moving).

Exceptions The only exceptions to this rule are the group of adjectives ending in *-y* which are based on words ending in *-er*:

blister	:	*blistery*	*plaster*	:	*plastery*
bluster	:	*blustery*	*splinter*	:	*splintery*

and also *slippery*.

3. If what precedes the [əri] ending in a *noun* is recognizable as an English word, the ending is likely to be **-ery**; if it is not, the ending is likely to be **-ary** or **-ory**:

buffoon	:	*buffoonery*	*debauch*	:	*debauchery*
green	:	*greenery*	*tomfool*	:	*tomfoolery*

but *vocabulary* and *laboratory* (there are no words *vocabul* or *laborat* in English).

This rule applies equally to words in which predictable changes are made to the base-word such as doubling the final letter or dropping a final *e*:

distil	:	*distillery*	*pig* :	*piggery*
machine	:	*machinery*	*slave* :	*slavery*

Exceptions Among the words that do not fit in with this rule are:

dictionary	*missionary*	*tributary*
infirmary	*secretary*	*visionary*
legionary		

(with *a* where *e* would be expected) and

artillery	*dysentery*	*gallery*
cemetery	*effrontery*	

(with *e* where *a* or *o* might be expected).

Other exceptions are words like *accessory* and *directory*, which are covered by rule 4 below.

4. If by replacing the [*əri*] ending of a word by -*ion* another English word is formed, the [*əri*] ending is probably spelt with an *o*:

accession	:	*accessory*	*direction*	:	*directory*
migration	:	*migratory*	*provision*	:	*provisory*
satisfaction	:	*satisfactory*	*undulation*	:	*undulatory*

Many words which end in [*əri*] are not covered by the above guidelines. These must simply be learnt individually. If in doubt, consult a dictionary.

-c

In order to preserve the hard [*k*] sound of the letter *c*, words ending in *c* add a *k* before suffixes beginning with *e*, *i*, or *y*:

picnic : *picnicking* : *picnicked* : *picnicker*
frolic : *frolicking* : *frolicked*
colic : *colicky*
panic : *panicking* : *panicked* : *panicky*

Exceptions *Arc, talc* and *zinc* are exceptions to this rule:

arc : *arcing* : *arced*

talc : *talcing* or *talcking* : *talced* or *talcked* : *talcky*

zinc : *zincing, zincking* or *zinking* : *zincy, zincky* or *zinky*

Warning A *k* is, of course, not added when the [*k*] sound is not preserved:

domestic : *domesticity*   *italic* : *italicize*

capital letters

The correct use of capital letters is an important part of correct spelling. The rules for capitalization are not difficult:

1. Capital letters must be used at the beginning of every sentence.

2. Capitals are required for the first letter of the names of people, countries, etc., and of words derived from them:

John; Anne; Sir Bernard Smith;

Australia; the Australian cricket team;

South Africa; a South African plant;

Christ; Christian;

Chestnut Avenue;

the Bay of Bengal.

Exceptions Many words which are in origin proper names or are derived from proper names do not take a capital: *pasteurize, wellington, sandwich, watt, ampere.* The difference between these words and words in the category above is that these exceptions denote things named after people or places rather than referring to the people or places themselves.

In some cases, forms with and without capitals are equally correct: *plaster of paris/Paris; platonic/Platonic love.* If you are uncertain, consult a dictionary.

Warning Words which require a capital in names and titles do not of course need one in other circumstances: *the Republic of South Africa* but *South Africa is a republic; the President of the United States* (= a particular person) but

How many presidents of the United States have there been?;
South America but *the south of England.*

3. Capitals must be used for the first letter of all 'important' words in the titles of books, plays, people, organizations, and so on:
the Prince of Wales;
Admiral of the Fleet Lord Brown;
the Department of Health and Social Services;
a book entitled 'Big Fish'.

When a title is hyphenated, both parts have a capital letter: *Major-General Smith.*

Words that are not 'important' are *a/an, the,* conjunctions like *and, as, but, if, when* and prepositions such as *at, in, of, off, on, with.*

Exception The first word of a book's or play's title must always have a capital letter, even if it is one of the small 'unimportant' words:
This book is called 'The Biggest Fish in the World'.

two points to note

1. Seasons should not normally have capitals, but it may occasionally be necessary to write *Spring* rather than *spring* for the sake of clarity.

2. *Sir, madam,* etc. should always have a capital at the beginning of a letter: *Dear Sir.*

-ce, -se, -cy, -sy

Should one write *defence* or *defense, practice* or *practise*? If *offence* is correct, is the related adjective spelt *offencive* or *offensive*? There are, unfortunately, few general rules to help the writer, but the following points are worth noting:

1. Words which are pronounced with a [z] sound are written with an *s*: *advise, devise, exercise, expertise, refuse* (verb), *revise, treatise,* etc. (But also ⇒ **-ise, -ize**.)

2. Words which are pronounced with an [s] sound

immediately following a vowel are generally written with a *c*: *advice, deduce, device, justice, lice, mice, office, rejoice, voice*, etc.

Exceptions Among the exceptions to this rule are *house, louse, mouse, obtuse, profuse, promise, refuse* (noun).

Note also the spelling of the noun *prophecy* and the related verb *prophesy*.

3. Nouns which are related to adjectives ending in *-ant* or *-ent* are written with a *c*:

different : *difference   ignorant* : *ignorance*

The same holds for nouns ending in *y*, and for other nouns related to verbs in any of the ways listed in the article **-ance, -ence**:

account : *accountancy   constant* : *constancy*
guide   : *guidance   interfere* : *interference*

4. Adjectives ending in [*ens*] are spelt with an *s*:

dense, immense, intense, tense.

Other words which are pronounced with an [*s*] sound following a consonant might have either *c* or *s* in writing.

Among words written with *c* are:

advance	*dance*	*hence*	*romance*
commence	*fence*	*pence*	*since*
commerce	*finance*	*pronounce*	

Among the words written with an *s* are:

endorse	*recompense*	*response* *sense*

American English and British English

The above rules apply in both British and American English. However, there are a number of words in which these two forms of English differ in usage:

In British English, *licence* and *practice* are nouns, *license* and *practise* the related verbs. In American English, the forms *license* and *practice* are used for both the noun and the verb. In British English, the nouns *defence, offence* and *pretence* are spelt with a c, but in American English they are written with an *s*. Note that the related adjectives *defensive* and *offensive* are written with an *s* in both British and American English.

The noun *vice* (= a fault or bad habit) is written with *c* in both American and British English, but *vice* (= a tool with metal jaws for holding things firmly) is written with *c* in British English and *s* in American English.

-cede, -ceed, -sede

Most words ending in [*sēd*] are spelt **-cede**. The only three words which end in **-ceed** are *exceed, proceed* and *succeed*. Only *supersede* ends in **-sede**.

-ch, -tch

A frequent spelling error is the omission of the *t* before *ch* in words like *dispatch* or the insertion of a *t* in words like *attach* and *detach*.

The best way to deal with this problem is to learn the general rule which covers most cases, and then to note and try to learn the exceptions to the rule. The rule is as follows:

If what precedes the [*ch*] sound is a consonant, [*ch*] will be written *ch*:

arch	church	search	touch
branch	filch	squelch	zilch

If what precedes the [*ch*] sound is a vowel written with a single letter, [*ch*] will be written *tch*:

catch	fetch	scratch	watch
dispatch	hutch	vetch	witch

If what precedes the [*ch*] is a vowel written with more than one letter, the spelling will be *ch*:

approach	couch	mooch	teach
brooch	debauch	screech	touch

89

Exceptions A number of very common words do not obey this rule, having *ch* where *tch* would be expected; but they are few in number and easily memorized:

attach	*ostrich*	*spinach*
detach	*rich*	*such*
enrich	*sandwich*	*which*
much		

One word, the name of the letter *h*, is an exception to the rule about double-letter vowels, being spelt *aitch* with a *t* where no *t* would be expected.

-cion, -tion, -sion see -tion, -sion, -cion.

-ction, -xion

Most words ending in [*-ak′shən*], [*-ek′shən*], [*-ik′shən*], etc. are spelt **-ction**:

action	*conviction*	*fraction*	*protection*
benediction	*defection*	*friction*	*putrefaction*
collection	*deflection*	*infection*	*reflection*
conduction	*dejection*	*inflection*	*resurrection*
confection	*direction*	*inspection*	*satisfaction*
connection	*distraction*	*instruction*	*section*
construction	*election*	*introduction*	*subtraction*
contraction	*erection*	*production*	*transaction*
contradiction	*fiction*		

Similarly, with an *n* before the *c*:

conjunction   *disjunction*   *distinction*   *extinction*

In British English, but not American English, four of the words in the above list may be written **-xion**:

connexion   *deflexion*   *inflexion*   *reflexion*

The **-ction** forms are now commoner than the **-xion** forms, but some people still prefer the forms *connexion* and *inflexion*.

Warning A few words *must* be written **-xion**. Among these are *complexion, crucifixion, genuflexion, transfixion*.

-cy, -sy see -acy, -asy and -ce, -se, -cy, -sy.

-dge

In most cases, the final *e* of words ending in **-dge** (such as *hedge, fridge, knowledge*) is dropped before suffixes beginning with *e, i* or *y*, but retained before suffixes beginning with *a, o, u* or a consonant:

judged : *judging*
dodger : *dodges* : *dodgy*
drudgery : *drudgism*
knowledgeable

Before the ending *-ment*, however, the *e* may equally correctly be dropped or retained:

judgment or *judgement*
acknowledgment or *acknowledgement*

Formerly, the forms without the *e* were standard, but now the forms with the *e* retained are more common.

Notice also the spelling of the word *fledgling*, with the final *e* of *fledge* dropped, contrary to what one might expect.

double consonants within words

A common error is the writing of a single instead of a double letter in words such as *misspell, really, illegible,* and *unnecessary.* If, however, you think for a moment how such words are made up, and consider the spelling of each part of the words separately, no such mistakes should occur:

misspell	= *mis* (= 'wrongly')	+ *spell*
unnecessary	= *un* (= 'not')	+ *necessary*
illegible	= *il* (= 'not')	+ *legible*
immortal	= *im* (= 'not')	+ *mortal*
dissatisfaction	= *dis* (= 'not')	+ *satisfaction*
really	= *real*	+ *ly*
suddenness	= *sudden*	+ *ness*
drunkenness	= *drunken*	+ *ness*

doubling of final consonants

There can be few English-speakers who are unaware that the

final consonant of many words is doubled when a suffix (or 'word-ending') is added:

drop : *dropping* : *dropped*
forget : *unforgettable*
grit : *gritty*
big : *bigger* : *biggest*
council : *councillor*
occur : *occurrence*
leg : *leggings*
god : *goddess*
glad : *gladden*
red : *reddish*

and so on. The problem for some people is that in many apparently similar words, the final consonant is *not* doubled before a suffix:

sleep : *sleeping*
dream : *dreaming*
gossip : *gossiping* : *gossipy*
common : *commoner* : *commonest*
visit : *visitor*
green : *greenish*
prefer : *preference*

and so on.

This problem only arises with suffixes which begin with a vowel (*a, e, i, o, u* or *y*). If the suffix begins with a consonant, the final consonant of the base word is never doubled:

equip : *equipment*   *spot* : *spotless*
sin : *sinful*   *chief* : *chiefly*

For suffixes which begin with a vowel, the rule is fairly straight-forward but does require a little bit of thought. It runs as follows:

If the base word ends in a single consonant, if the consonant is preceded by a single vowel-sound written with a single letter, and if the vowel is stressed, then the final consonant is doubled; if any one of these conditions is not met, then the consonant is not doubled.

This perhaps sounds a bit complicated, but it is really quite simple, as a few examples will show:

i) *Begin* ends with a single consonant, *n*; the consonant is preceded by a single vowel-sound, [*i*], which is written with a single letter, *i*; and the word is stressed (that is, it has its strongest or loudest point) on the *i*. The three conditions for doubling the *n* before a suffix beginning with a vowel are met, and the words *beginner* and *beginning* are therefore correctly spelt with a double *n*.

ii) *Visit* ends in a single consonant, preceded by a single vowel-sound written with a single letter, but is stressed on the first syllable, not on the vowel before the *t* ([*viz´it*]) and therefore does not fulfil one of the necessary conditions for the *t* to be doubled. A single *t* is therefore correct in *visited*, *visiting*, and *visitor*.

iii) The word *plan* ends in a single consonant, which is preceded by a single-letter vowel *a*. Is the vowel stressed? Since there is only one vowel in this word, it must be. The conditions for doubling the final consonant are therefore all met, so the *n* is correctly doubled in *planned*, *planner*, and *planning*.

iv) The vowel-sound of *dream*, [*ē*], is written with two letters, *ea*, not a single letter. One of the conditions for doubling the final consonant is thus not met, and the final *m* is therefore not doubled in *dreamed*, *dreamer*, *dreaming*, and *dreamy*.

There are two points that should be noted:

1. A *u* following a *q* counts as part of a consonant, so the final consonant in a word such as *quit* is treated as being preceded by a single vowel, not two vowels. The *t* is therefore correctly doubled in *quitter* and *quitting*.

2. Notice that even if a consonant is not pronounced, it usually still counts as a consonant for the purposes of the

rule we are considering here. For example, the final *n* of *condemn* is not pronounced, nor is the *l* of *calm* or the *gh* of *light*. But even though we only *pronounce* a single consonant-sound at the end of these words, in their written form they end in <u>two</u> consonants, and the final consonant is therefore not doubled before a suffix:

condemn : *condemned* : *condemning*
calm : *calmer* : *calmest* : *calming*
light : *lighter* : *lightest* : *lighting*

A silent *h*, however, as in *hoorah*, does not count as a consonant, and is not doubled:

hoorahed : *hoorahing*

A final *y* or *w* which is part of the written form of a vowel-sound, as in *enjoy* or *allow*, does not count as a consonant either, and is not doubled:

enjoyed : *enjoying* : *enjoyable*
allowed : *allowing* : *allowable*

As you have seen, the basic rules for doubling final consonants are quite simple. There are, unfortunately, a number of exceptions, and exceptions to the exceptions:

x

x is pronounced [*ks*], and counts as two consonants, not one. The final *x* of *box* is therefore not doubled in *boxed*, *boxer*, *boxes*, and *boxing*.

Similarly with *fixed*, *fixing*; *relaxed*, *relaxing*; *sexes*, *sexy*; *mixed*, *mixer*, *mixes*, *mixing*, and so on.

c

A final *c* does not double but becomes *ck*:

picnic : *picnicker* : *picnicking*

l

A final *l* preceded by a single vowel-sound written with a single letter is doubled before *-ing*, *-ed*, *-er/-or*, *-ery*, *-ance/-ence*,

-ation/-ion, *-ious/-ous*, and *-y* irrespective of the stress pattern of the word. Hence one has not only

appal'	: *appalling*	: *appalled*		
rebel'	: *rebelling*	: *rebelled*	: *rebellion*	: *rebellious*
propel'	: *propelling*	: *propelled*	: *propellor*	: *propellant*

which follow the general rule, but also

sig'nal	: *signalling*	: *signalled*	: *signaller*
coun'sel	: *counselling*	: *counselled*	: *counsellor*
jew'el	: *jeweller*	: *jewellery*	
e'qual	: *equalling*	: *equalled*	
grav'el	: *gravelly*		
mar'vel	: *marvelled*	: *marvelling*	: *marvellous*
can'cel	: *cancelling*	: *cancelled*	: *cancellation*

Note The verb *parallel* is an exception to this rule. The final *l* does not double in *paralleling* and *paralleled*.

Some adjectives ending in *-ous* do not have a double *l*:

miraculous	*querulous*	*scandalous*
perilous	*ridiculous*	*scurrilous*
populous		

Before the suffixes *-ise/-ize*, *-ism*, *-ist*, and *-ity*, the final *l* is not doubled:

equal	: *equalise*	: *equality*	
special	: *specialise*	: *specialist*	: *speciality*
final	: *finalise*	: *finalist*	: *finality*
civil	: *civilise*		

Note Here again there are exceptions:

crystal	: *crystallise*	(and also *crystalline*)
tranquil	: *tranquillise*	: *tranquillity*
medal	: *medallist*	
panel	: *panellist*	

Notice the spelling of *tonsillitis*, much more common than *tonsilitis*, although both forms are correct.

If the vowel before the *l* is written with a double letter, *l* is not doubled (which is to say, *l* follows the general rule):

sail : *sailor*

fool : *fooling* : *fooled*

Note, however, the spelling of *woollen* and *woolly* with unpredictable doubled *l*'s.

p

Most verbs which end in *p* follow the general rule, but three common ones do not, doubling the final *p* where according to the stress-pattern one would not expect it:

wor′ship : *worshipping* : *worshipped* : *worshipper*

kid′nap : *kidnapping* : *kidnapped* : *kidnapper*

han′dicap : *handicapping* : *handicapped*

-fer

Words ending in *-fer* (e.g. *confer, prefer*) follow the general rules for the most part. Note that when such words are followed by *-able* and *-ence*, the stress moves from the *-fer* to the first syllable, and the *r* is therefore not doubled:

prefer : *preferring* but *preferable* : *preference*

confer : *conferring* but *conference*

Exceptions Note that in *inferable* and *transferable* the stress remains on *-fer*, but that nonetheless the *r* is not doubled.

-gram

Words ending in *-gram* double the final *m*:

program : *programmed* : *programming* : *programmable*

diagram : *diagrammatic*

compound words

A compound word is one which is made up of two or more shorter words, e.g. *blackboard* (= *black* + *board*) or *snowman* (= *snow* + *man*). No matter what the stress pattern of the word is, the final consonant of a compound word is doubled if, in accordance with the rules we have stated above, it would be doubled when not in a compound. For example:

whip : *whipped* : *whipping*

horsewhip : *horsewhipped* : *horsewhipping*

even though the stress in *horsewhip* is on *horse*, not *whip*.

A number of other words behave as if they were compounds and double the final letter contrary to what would be expected from the general rule:

humbug : *humbugging* : *humbugged*

leapfrog : *leapfrogging* : *leapfrogged*

zigzag : *zigzagging* : *zigzagged*

hobnob : *hobnobbing* : *hobnobbed*

and finally . . .

Some words allow both single and doubled consonants, e.g. *focus, focusing* or *focussing*. To add to the problem, nouns and verbs sometimes behave differently in this respect! Note the following:

bias	noun plural *biases*
	verb parts with either single or double *s*
bus	noun plural usually *buses*, but *busses* also correct, although rare
	verb usually with single *s* but *ss* also correct
focus	noun plural *focuses*
	verb parts with single or double *s*
gas	noun plural *gases*
	verb *gasses* : *gassing* : *gassed*
	Note also *gaseous* and *gasify*
plus	plural *pluses* or *plusses*
yes	plural *yeses* or *yesses*

-e

There is a general rule for words ending in *e* which applies to nouns, verbs, adjectives and adverbs alike. The rule is as follows:

when adding a suffix (or 'word-ending') beginning with a vowel to a word which ends in *e*, drop the *e*; when adding a suffix which begins with a consonant, do not drop the *e*.
Examples of these are easy to find:

change : *changing*
move : *moving* : *movement*
guide : *guidance*
admire : *admirable* : *admiration* : *admirer* : *admired*
culture : *cultural*
concise : *concisely* : *conciseness*
use : *useful* : *useless*
bone : *bony*
desire : *desirous* : *desirable*
awe : *awesome*
safe : *safety*

There are a number of exceptions to this general rule, some predictable and some not.

-ce, -ge

In order to preserve the 'soft' sound of *c* and *g* (i.e. [*s*] and [*j*]), the *e* is not dropped before a suffix beginning with *a*, *o* or *u*:

change : *changeable*   *peace* : *peaceable*
courage : *courageous*   *knowledge*: *knowledgeable*

-ie

Verbs which end in *-ie* change this to *y* before *-ing*:

belie : *belying*
die : *dying*   *lie* : *lying*
tie : *tying*   *vie* : *vying*

-oe, -ee, -ye

Verbs ending in *oe*, *ee*, and *ye* keep the final *e* before all suffixes except those beginning with an *e*:

hoe : *hoeing* : *hoed*
shoe : *shoeing*
agree : *agreeing* : *agreed* : *agreeable*

eye : *eyeing*

dye : *dyeing* (compare *dying* from the verb *die*)

singe, etc.
A final *e* is retained before *-ing* where necessary to distinguish between words that would otherwise be indistinguishable: compare *sing* : *singing* and *singe* : *singeing*. Similarly one writes *routeing*, *swingeing*, and *tingeing*.

-le
Adjectives which end in *-le* preceded by one or more consonants do not add *-ly* to form adverbs but replace the *e* by *y*:

double	:	*doubly*	*simple*	:	*simply*
subtle	:	*subtly*	*supple*	:	*supply*

-y
The final *e* is retained before *-y* in words that end in *ue* (e.g. *glue* : *gluey*), and also unpredictably in a small number of other words:

cage	:	*cagey*	*pace*	:	*pacey*
dice	:	*dicey*	*price*	:	*pricey*
mate	:	*matey*		

Both *nosy* and *nosey* are correct. Notice the difference in spelling between *holy* (= sacred) and *holey* (= full of holes).

and finally . . .
There remains a mixed bag of exceptions which one must simply list and learn.

Four adjectives which end in *e* have unpredictably spelt adverb forms:

due	:	*duly*	*eerie*	:	*eerily*
true	:	*truly*	*whole*	:	*wholly*

The spelling of the following words must also be noted:

awful, not *aweful*
ninth, not *nineth*
acreage, not *acrage*
ageism, not *agism*
fledgling, not *fledgeling*.

Some words allow both regular and irregular forms:

ageing or *aging*
cueing or *cuing*
mileage or *milage*
judgement or *judgment* (and similarly for other words ending in -*dgement*)
blameable or *blamable* (and similarly *lik(e)able*, *liv(e)able*, *lov(e)able*, *mov(e)able* and *siz(e)able*.

-e-, -ae- see -ae-, -e-.

-ed, -d

verbs

To form the past tense or past participle, most regular verbs add -*ed* to the base form:

walk	:	*walked*	*sail*	: *sailed*
toss	:	*tossed*	*toast*	: *toasted*
taxi	:	*taxied*	*veto*	: *vetoed*

If the base verb ends in an *e*, the *e* is dropped before -*ed* is added:

bake	: *baked*	*change*	: *changed*
agree	: *agreed*		

Verbs that end in *y* change the *y* to *i* if it is preceded by a consonant but not if it is preceded by a vowel:

cry	: *cried*	*stay*	: *stayed*

Exceptions Note that *laid*, *paid* and *said* are exceptions to this last rule.

For the doubling of final consonants in words such as *fit*, *fitted* and *drop*, *dropped* ⇒ **doubling of final consonants.**

Words which end in *c* generally add a *k* before -*ed*:

picnic : picnicked *panic : panicked*

For exceptions to this ⇒ **-c.**

adjectives

Adjectives ending in -*ed* and -*d* follow the same rules as the verbs:

red-haired *bearded* *long-legged*

leisured *good-natured*

Exceptions The adjective *moneyed* (= 'having money', 'rich') may also correctly be spelt *monied*.

-efy, -ify see **-ify, -efy.**

-ei-, -ie-

words pronounced with an [ē] sound

A well-known and very useful rule is the one which runs:

'*i* before *e* except after *c*'.

This rule applies only to words which are pronounced with an [ē] sound:

believe *chief* *siege*

ceiling *deceive* *receipt*

Exceptions A few common words pronounced with an [ē] sound have *ei* where *ie* would be expected:

caffeine *heinous* *protein* *skein*

codeine *inveigle* *seize* *weir*

counterfeit *neither* *sheikh* *weird*

either

Notice that some of these words (e.g. *either, heinous*) may be pronounced in more than one way and also appear in some of the lists in the sections below. Some names of people and places also do not obey the general rule:

Keith Neil Sheila Reid Madeira.

words that are not pronounced [ē]

1. When words of this type are pronounced with an [ā] sound, *ei* is always correct:

deign	*heir*	*reign*	*veil*
eight	*inveigh*	*rein*	*vein*
feign	*inveigle*	*sheikh*	*weigh*
freight	*neigh*	*skein*	*weight*
heinous	*neighbour*	*sleigh*	

and also the Chinese dish *chow mein*.

Spelling hint For this group of words, remember the spelling of *eight*, which most people spell correctly.

2. Words pronounced [ī] usually have *ei*:

either	*Fahrenheit*	*height*
leitmotif	*neither*	*seismograph*
sleight of hand		

However, before the letter *r*, *ie* is correct:

fiery	*hierarchy*	*hieroglyphics*

3. Following a *c* or a *t* which is pronounced [*sh*], *ie* is always correct:

ancient	*efficient*	*quotient*	*sufficient*
conscience	*patient*	*species*	

4. After the above rules have been grasped, there remain only a few more words which need to be learnt:

Handkerchief and *mischief* follow the spelling of *chief* (which is predictably *ie*), and *mischievous* follows the spelling of *mischief*.

Words ending in [*rin*] with a silent *g* follow the spelling of *reign* (which is predictably *ei*):

foreign   *sovereign*

Words ending in [*fit*] are spelt *ei*:

counterfeit   *forfeit*   *surfeit*

Heifer and *leisure* are spelt *ei* but *friend* with *ie* (notice as a spelling hint that *friend* ends in -*end*).

And that leaves *sieve*, with *ie*.

-ence, -ance see **-ance, -ence.**

-eous, -ious see **-ious, -eous.**

-er, -est

In general, **-er** and **-est** are added directly to adjectives and adverbs to form comparatives and superlatives:

hard	:	*harder*	:	*hardest*
fast	:	*faster*	:	*fastest*

There are, however, certain important spelling rules which must be observed in the formation of comparatives and superlatives:

1. When the adjective ends in *e*, the *e* is dropped before **-er** and **-est** are added:

white	:	*whiter*	:	*whitest*
simple	:	*simpler*	:	*simplest*

If the adjective ends in two *e*'s, one *e* is dropped:

free	:	*freer*	:	*freest*

2. If the adjective ends in a single consonant, if the vowel preceding that consonant is written with a single letter, and if the vowel and consonant are part of a stressed syllable, the consonant is doubled before **-er** and **-est**:

red	:	*redder*	:	*reddest*
big	:	*bigger*	:	*biggest*

A final *l* is doubled in any case:

cruel	:	*crueller*	:	*cruellest*

3. A final *y* preceded by a consonant changes to *i* before **-er** and **-est**:

funny	:	*funnier*	:	*funniest*
silly	:	*sillier*	:	*silliest*

Note In the case of certain one-syllable words in which the *y* is pronounced [*i*], both *y* and *i* are correct before **-er** and **-est**:

shy :	*shyer* or *shier*	:	*shyest* or *shiest*
sly :	*slyer* or *slier*	:	*slyest* or *sliest*
wry :	*wryer* or *wrier*	:	*wryest* or *wriest*

In the case of *dry, drier* and *driest* are the preferred forms.
In the case of *spry, spryer* and *spryest* are preferred.
A final *y* preceded by a vowel remains as *y* (*grey, greyer,
greyest*), unless it is part of an adjective ending in *-ey* which
has been formed from a noun (e.g. *clayey* from *clay*, *matey*
from *mate*), in which case the *ey* changes to *i*:

clayey : *clayier* : *clayiest*
matey : *matier* : *matiest*

-er, -or, -ar

-er

The suffix **-er** can be added to verbs in English to form nouns
meaning 'someone or something that ——s': *singer, builder,
worker, talker*, etc. There is virtually no limit to the number of
nouns which can be created in this way.

There is, in addition, a small group of **-er** nouns that are
based on other nouns or on adjectives rather than on verbs:

foreigner	*lawyer*	*sorcerer*
idolater	*mariner*	*treasurer*
jeweller	*prisoner*	*usurer*

-or

There are a large number of 'doer' words which end in **-or**. The
following are the ones most likely to be met with:

accelerator	*constructor*	*educator*	*legislator*
actor	*contractor*	*elevator*	*mediator*
administrator	*contributor*	*escalator*	*microprocessor*
arbitrator	*councillor*	*excavator*	*narrator*
auditor	*counsellor*	*executor*	*navigator*
calculator	*creator*	*governor*	*objector*
collaborator	*decorator*	*incubator*	*operator*
collector	*depositor*	*indicator*	*oppressor*
commentator	*dictator*	*inheritor*	*orator*
competitor	*director*	*inspector*	*perpetrator*
conductor	*distributor*	*inventor*	*professor*
conqueror	*duplicator*	*investigator*	*projector*
conspirator	*editor*	*investor*	*prospector*

protector	sailor	surveyor	vendor
radiator	spectator	survivor	ventilator
refrigerator	supervisor	translator	visitor

Spelling hint As a possible clue to the **-or** spelling, notice how many of the words in the above list end in *-ator*, *-itor* and *-utor*, and notice also that many of those ending in *-tor* are related to words ending in *-tion*:

collector : *collection*	*oppressor* : *oppression*
objector : *objection*	*supervisor* : *supervision*

There are a few other words, not related to verbs, which end in **-or**:

ambassador	creditor	janitor	sponsor
ancestor	curator	major	successor
author	debtor	mayor	suitor
aviator	doctor	pastor	tailor
bachelor	emperor	predecessor	tenor
benefactor	equator	proprietor	tractor
captor	impostor	rector	traitor
censor	inquisitor	senator	victor
chancellor	jailor	solicitor	

Warning Some words have both **-or** and **-er** forms, e.g. *carburettor, carburetter.*

Both *caster* and *castor* are correct for the device in sprinkling sugar, and for a small wheel, but *castor* is the commoner. And both *conjurer* and *conjuror* are correct.

In some cases, the two nouns differ slightly in meaning:

adapter, adaptor	*conveyer, conveyor*
resister, resistor	

In such cases, the **-er** word is more general in meaning ('one who——s'), while the **-or** word is more specialized or technical in meaning (*adaptor* and *resistor* are pieces of electrical apparatus; *conveyor* = 'conveyor-belt').

-ar

Some common 'doer' words are spelt **-ar**:

| beggar | bursar | pedlar | scholar |
| burglar | liar | registrar | vicar |

Other common **-ar** nouns are:

altar	cellar	guitar	pillar
calendar	collar	hangar	vinegar
caterpillar	dollar	mortar	
cedar	grammar	nectar	

adjectives

Adjectives ending in [ər] are usually spelt **-ar**:

angular	molar	perpendicular	singular
circular	molecular	polar	spectacular
familiar	muscular	popular	stellar
insular	particular	regular	tubular
jocular	peculiar	similar	vulgar
lunar			

When any of these words is used as a noun, the ending is still **-ar**.

Spelling hint Notice as a clue for the **-ar** spelling that many of the above list are related to nouns ending in **-arity** in which the *a* is fully pronounced.

circul̲a̲r : *circul̲a̲rity*   *popul̲a̲r* : *popul̲a̲rity*

A small group of adjectives (some of which are again used as nouns) end in **-or**. These are:

major	minor	inferior	superior
interior	exterior	anterior	ulterior
tenor			

Spelling hint As with the **-ar** group listed above, these **-or** words are often related to words ending in **-ority** (*minor*: *minority*) in which the *o* is fully sounded.

There are some fairly predictable spelling rules which must be observed in the formation of words ending in **-er**, **-or** and **-ar**:

final *e*

The final *e* of a verb drops before the ending is added:

bake	:	baker	contribute	:	contributor
burgle	:	burglar	manage	:	manager
lie	:	liar			

final *y*

A final *y* preceded by a consonant becomes *i*; a *y* preceded by a vowel remains as *y*:

   carry : *carrier*   *survey* : *surveyor*

Note Both *flier* and *flyer*, and *drier* and *dryer*, are correct.

doubling of final consonants

A final consonant which would be doubled in the formation of the *-ed* and *-ing* forms of a verb doubles before **-er**, **-or** and **-ar** are added:

   begin : *beginning* : *beginner*
   beg : *begged* : *begging* : *beggar*
   counsel : *counselled* : *counselling* : *counsellor*

Even if there is no corresponding verb form, the rules set out in **doubling of final consonants** apply:

   council : *councillor*

final *c*

A final *c* adds *k* before **-er**:

   picnic : *picnicker*

See also the article **-or, -our** for the spelling of words such as *humour, colour* and *neighbour*.

-ery, -ary, -ory see **-ary, -ery, -ory.**

for-, fore-

The prefix **fore-** means 'before, in front, beforehand'. It is much commoner than **for-**, and there are a great many words beginning with **fore-**, among which are *forearm, foreboding, forecast, forefinger, forehead, foreman, forerunner, foresee, foreshadow, foresight, forestall, foretell,* and *forewarn.*

   The prefix **for-** means 'away', 'not', 'against', 'utterly', but it is not a living prefix (that is, it is no longer used to create new words) and its meaning is not always obvious in words which begin with it, such as *forget* and *forgive.* Other common words beginning with **for-** are *forbear* (verb), *forbid*, *forfeit*, *forgo*, *forlorn*, *forsake*, and *forswear*.

Spelling hint   As a general rule, when in doubt, think whether or not the word you want to spell has anything to do with the notion 'before, in front': if it has, the spelling will be **-fore**; if it hasn't, the spelling should be **for-**. One exception is *foreclose*, in which one would, by the above rule, expect the spelling **for-**.

Warning   A few of the words beginning with **for-** and **fore-** are very similar, and especial attention must be paid to these: to *forbear* is 'not to do (something)', a *forebear* is 'an ancestor' (the spelling *forbear* is also correct); to *forgo* means 'to do without (something)', a *foregone conclusion* is 'an obvious or inevitable conclusion'. Notice also the difference in spelling between the *foreword* of a book and the adverb *forward*.

hyphen

compound words

For many people, hyphenation is one of the greatest headache-creating aspects of English spelling. However, although there are certain word-types—in particular, compound nouns—in which hyphenation does not seem to follow any logical or consistent rule, there are many categories of word in which the rules are fairly clear-cut and consistent, if not entirely so, and therefore quite simple to follow.

In general, a hyphen is used to show that two or more words are to be treated as a single unit:

> *She is my mother-in-law*
> *A good-looking, hard-working boy*

In many cases, a hyphen is so used to avoid ambiguities: compare *a little-known writer* and *a little, known writer*; *200-odd people* (= about 200 people) and *200 odd people* (= 200 strange people).

The following are the most important rules of hyphenation:

1. A compound adjective consisting of two words, the second of which is a present or past participle or a word ending in *-ed*, is normally hyphenated:

good-natured	*hard-wearing*	*never-ending*
black-headed	*hard-hearted*	*panic-stricken*
card-carrying	*battle-scarred*	

When the first word of such a compound is one of the adverbs **well, better, best, ill, worse, worst**, a hyphen is inserted only when the compound adjective precedes a noun, not when it occupies other positions in the sentence: *a well-known author* but *He is well known as an author* and *Well known as an author, Jim Brown is now making a name for himself as an actor.*

A past or present participle preceded by an adverb ending in *-ly* is not linked to the adverb by a hyphen in any position in the sentence: *The room is beautifully decorated; a beautifully decorated room.* This rule may be broken if a hyphen is needed for the sake of clarity.

2. Nouns formed from phrasal verbs (i.e. a verb plus *in, out, off,* etc.) are generally hyphenated:

take-over	*fly-past*	*going-over*
shake-up	*share-out*	*passer-by*

A few such nouns may be written without a hyphen (e.g. *layout, hideout, stopover*), but a hyphen is not incorrect, so whenever you are in doubt, put one in.

Warning A hyphen should not be used to join the parts of a phrasal verb itself: *We will have to share out the money,* not *. . . share-out the money.* Notice the difference between *His going-over* (noun) *of the accounts was very thorough* and *His going over* (verb plus preposition) *the accounts caused a lot of problems.*

3. Phrases of various types, when used as adjectives and preceding the noun they qualify, require hyphens:
an up-to-date report
a balance-of-payments problem
our next-door neighbours
a never-to-be-forgotten experience

4. Numbers from 21 to 99 and fractions should be hyphenated:

twenty-three   *fifty-six*   *one-third*

5. Compound adjectives consisting of two simple adjectives or a noun plus an adjective are usually hyphenated when preceding a noun and often (but not always) hyphenated in other positions (e.g. after the verb *be*):

a pitch-dark night
It's pitch-dark outside
blood-red wine

6. In the case of compound nouns, a comparison of the entries in two or more dictionaries will show that there are many words in which hyphenation usage is not clearly established: *coal gas* or *coal-gas*; *fire-guard* or *fireguard*. In general, a compound noun is written as two words if it is felt that the first word simply qualifies the second word like an adjective, but as a hyphenated word or a single word with no hyphen if the compound is felt to be a single lexical item denoting a particular thing or type of thing:

a bus company, trade figures but *bus-driver, trademark*.

If the 'single lexical item' type of word is well established and frequently used, and is built up from one-syllable words, it is likely to be written as a single word with no hyphen:

bedroom; *bloodbath*; *teacup*.

A hyphen is more likely in longer words, and where the absence of a hyphen would allow an undesirable or confusing juxtaposition of sounds or letters:

heart-throb rather than *heartthrob*
pole-axe rather than *poleaxe*
time-exposure rather than *timeexposure*.

7. Prefixes like *un-*, *dis-*, *mis-*, *pre-* and *re-* are not normally followed by a hyphen. However, if the word to which a prefix is added begins with a capital letter, a hyphen is inserted:

un-American; *un-English*

Note also the use of a hyphen to distinguish *re-cover* (to cover again) from *recover* (to become well again), *re-count* (to count again) from *recount* (to tell), and so on, and to avoid the juxtaposition of two *e*'s in *re-enter*, *re-elect*, etc.

Ex- and *non-* are normally followed by a hyphen:
ex-wife; *non-inflammable*

Compound words formed with *half-* and *self-* are generally hyphenated:
half-brother; *half-term*; *self-respect*
Exceptions *Halfpenny* and *halfway* are two exceptions.

Words beginning with *co-* need not have a hyphen, but if the letter following the *co-* is an *o*, a hyphen is preferable:
co-exist or *coexist*; *co-operation*; *co-opt*

Anti- is generally not followed by a hyphen:
anticlockwise; *antifreeze*
A few words are, however, hyphenated:
anti-hero; *anti-marketeer*
(See the list at **ante-, anti-**.)

8. The suffixes *-fold*, *-ish*, *-most*, *-ness*, *-ship* and *-wise* are not normally preceded by a hyphen:

tenfold	*innermost*	*kingship*
greenish	*meanness*	*lengthwise*

word-breaks
Hyphens are used to mark breaks in words not normally hyphenated, either when only part of the word is written, as in *four- or fivefold*, (where *four-* represents 'fourfold'), or at the end of a line of writing where part of the word has to be taken over to the next line. In the latter case, the following rules apply:

1. If possible, split the word into logical parts in such a way that the former part suggests the whole word, or at least does not mislead the reader by suggesting the wrong word:
mis-/shapen not *miss-/hapen* or *misshap-/en*
re-/install, not *rein-/stall*
heat-/ing, not *he-/ating*

2. A letter that influences the pronunciation of another letter should not be separated from it at a line-break:

spe-/cial not *spec-/ial*

magi-/cian not *magic-/ian*

-ible see -able, -ible.

-ie-, -ei- see -ei-, -ie-.

-ie, -y see -y, -ie.

-ify, -efy

Most words ending in [*ifī*] are spelt *-ify*:

classify	*horrify*	*notify*
exemplify	*identify*	*simplify*
falsify	*mystify*	*solidify*

and so on.

Four common words end in *-efy*:

liquefy	*putrefy*	*rarefy*	*stupefy*

ill-, imm-, inn-, irr-

The prefixes **il-**, **im-**, **in-**, **ir-** mostly occur in English words which are derived from Latin. They carry either the meaning 'not, opposite of' or the meaning 'in, into, on':

illegal	= 'not legal'
impossible	= 'not possible'
inaccurate	= 'not accurate'
irrelevant	= 'not relevant
immigration	= 'migration into (a country)'
innate	= 'in-born'

ill-, imm-, -irr

Any word beginning [*il*], [*im*] or [*ir*] which has the meaning 'not something' or 'in/into/on something' will have a double *l*, *m*, or *r*. This in fact covers the great majority of English words beginning [*il*], [*im*] or [*ir*] including ones in which the 'not' or 'in/into/on' notion is no longer obvious, e.g. *immense* (= so large as to be *not* measurable), *illuminate* (= to shine light *on* something), *irrigate* (= to put water *on* seeds and plants).

inn-, in-
Words beginning with [*in*] pose more of a problem as, in order to be certain how many *n*'s to write, you have to know whether the *in-* has been added to a base-word beginning with *n* or one beginning with a vowel, and sometimes you would need a knowledge of Latin to know this. There are some guidelines, however, that cover most cases:

1. If what follows the [*in*] is recognizable as an English word which begins with a vowel, or is clearly related to an English word beginning with a vowel, only one *n* is needed:

accurate	: *inaccurate*	*audible*	: *inaudible*
exact	: *inexact*	*offensive*	: *inoffensive*

2. If what follows the [*in*] is recognizable as an English word, or something clearly related to an English word, which begins with an *n*, two *n*'s are needed:

numerous : *innumerable* (= *not* countable)
novelty : *innovation* (= that which is brought *in* as something new)

There are in fact very few words with a double *n*; in addition to *innumerable* and *innovation*, the only ones you are likely to come across are *innate*, *innocent*, and *innuendo*.
Note A double *n* is needed also in a few words derived not from the Latin prefix *in-* but from English *in*: *innards*, *inner*, and *innings*.

-ing
The present participle of a verb is generally formed by adding **-ing** to the base-form:

walk	: *walking*	*sing* : *singing*
stay	: *staying*	

spelling points to note

1. Verbs ending in *e* drop the *e* before adding **-ing**:

bake : *baking*   *refine* : *refining*
queue : *queuing*

Exceptions Verbs ending in *ee*, *oe* and *ye* are exceptions to this rule, and do not drop the final *e*:

agree : *agreeing*   *hoe* : *hoeing*   *dye* : *dyeing*

A few words retain the final *e* in order to be distinguishable from similar words with no *e*. Compare *singe* : *singeing* and *sing* : *singing*. Similarly one writes *routeing*, *swingeing*, and *tingeing*.

One or two words may correctly be written with or without the *e*:

age : *ageing* or *aging*
cue : *cueing* or *cuing*

Verbs ending in *ie* alter this to *y* before adding **-ing**:

die : *dying*   *tie* : *tying*

2. Present participles of verbs obey the general rules for the doubling of final consonants before suffixes which are outlined in the article **doubling of final consonants**:

run : *running*   *swim* : *swimming*
prefer : *preferring*   *signal* : *signalling*
worship : *worshipping*   *zigzag* : *zigzagging*
For more details, see this article.

3. Words ending in *c*
Verbs ending in *c* generally add a *k* before **-ing**:
picnic : *picnicking*   *mimic* : *mimicking*
For the exceptions to this rule, see the article **-c**.

4. Verbs ending in *i*
ski : *skiing*   *taxi* : *taxiing* or *taxying*

-ious, -eous

Most words which end in [*iəs*] are spelt **-ious**:

abstemious	*glorious*	*oblivious*	*tedious*
copious	*imperious*	*spurious*	*various*

A small number of words are spelt **-eous**:

beauteous	erroneous	miscellaneous
bounteous	extraneous	nauseous
consanguineous	heterogeneous	piteous
contemporaneous	hideous	plenteous
courteous	homogeneous	simultaneous
discourteous	instantaneous	spontaneous
duteous		

Apart from these words, there are only a few technical words such as *aqueous* and *vitreous*.

The same general picture applies to words ending in [*shəs*], [*chəs*] and [*jəs*]. Most are spelt **-ious**:

atrocious	infectious	scrumptious
gracious	religious	

A few words are spelt **-eous**:

curvaceous	gorgeous	predaceous	righteous

In addition to these, there are the words ending in the suffix **-ous** in which the *e* of the base-word has been retained in order to preserve the soft *g* sound:

advantageous courageous outrageous

There are also a large number of technical and scientific words ending in **-aceous**, such as *herbaceous*.

ir-, irr- see Ill-, imm-, inn-, irr-.

-ise, -ize

Many verbs in English may be spelt **-ise** or **-ize**, e.g. *equalise/equalize; terrorise/terrorize*. There are some, however, which must always be spelt **-ise**, e.g. *advertise, despise, televise*. The problem is to remember which group a particular verb belongs to. The following guidelines may be of some help:

1. If the final syllable of the verb is not pronounced [*īz*], it will be written with an *s*:

promise, braise, praise, raise, reprise (pronounced [*ri-prēz′*])

2. If the **-ise** is part of the root (or 'core') of the verb rather than a suffix or 'word-ending' added to the root, it will be written with an *s*. The following are all the words in this category that you are likely to meet:

advertise	*comprise*	*exercise*	*rise*
advise	*compromise*	*franchise*	*supervise*
apprise	*despise*	*improvise*	*surmise*
arise	*devise*	*incise*	*surprise*
chastise	*disguise*	*premise*	*televise*
circumcise	*excise*	*revise*	

Spelling hint   Verbs ending in *-cise*, *-mise*, *-prise* and *-vise* are very likely to belong to this group if what precedes the *-ise* is not recognizable as an English word: there is, for example, no word *desp* or *superv* in English.

3. If the **-ise** is added to another English word as a suffix, it may equally correctly be written **-ize**:
critic : *criticise/criticize*
item : *itemise/itemize*
modern : *modernise/modernize*
victim : *victimise/victimize*

While for words of this category both **-ise** and **-ize** are correct, it should be noted that **-ise** is still the commoner of the two in British English whilst **-ize** is standard in American English.

Note   When the base word ends in an *e*, this *e* is dropped (as one would expect—see **-e**):
fertile : *fertilise/fertilize*
oxide : *oxidise/oxidize*

The verbs *crystallise/crystallize* and *tranquillise/tranquillize* have an unpredictable double *l* (compare *equalise*, *specialise*, etc.).

Warning   In some cases, the **-ise/-ize** ending is added not to a full word but to a word-root (the 'core' of a word which is left

when some other suffix has been removed):
antagonism : *antagonise/antagonize*
baptism : *baptise/baptize*
exorcism : *exorcise/exorcize*
harmony, harmonic : *harmonise/harmonize*
ostracism : *ostracise/ostracize*
sympathy, sympathetic : *sympathise/sympathize*

In a few cases, the word-root changes slightly in form:
synthetic : *synthesise/synthesize*

These words differ from those of section 2 above in that here the **-ise/-ize** is <u>added to the word-root</u> whereas in the words in section 2 the **-ise** is <u>part of the word-root</u> (to which other suffixes may be added, e.g. *revise*: *revision*).

Problems There are, unfortunately, a few problem words which do not quite fit into the general rules. *Advertise* and *chastise* look as if they belong in section 3 but in fact belong in the list of words in section 2, and must never be written with a *z*.

Recognise, maximise, minimise, optimise and *pulverise* look as they belong in section 2, but can be equally correctly written with *z*. Similarly *appetising* and *appetizing* are both correct.

Capsize must always be written with a *z*.

Merchandise as a noun is always written with an *s*, but may be written with *s* or *z* as a verb, the **-ise** form being by far the commoner.

Prize in the sense of 'award' is spelt with a *z*, but in the sense of 'to force open with a lever' may be spelt with *s* or *z*, and the *s*-form is the commoner of the two.

-yse

A very few words are spelt **-yse**, not **-ise**:
analyse, breathalyse, paralyse, psychoanalyse.

These words are always spelt with an *s* in British English. In American English, they are always spelt with a *z*.

-l, -ll

The letter *l* poses many spelling problems in English. One of the main ones is whether to write one or two *l*'s at the end of the word: for example *nil*, *annul*, *instil* and *appal* have one *l*, whereas *fill*, *dull*, and *install* have two. There are, fortunately, a few guidelines which will help you to get the spelling right.

If the word is only one syllable long and the vowel is a single letter, the chances are that the word will end with a double *l*:

all	chill	full	thrall
bill	dull	ill	toll
call	fell	mill	will

Exceptions There are very few exceptions, the only common ones being *gel*, *nil*, *pal* and *gal* (= girl).

The *ll* spelling is of course retained in compound words based on *call*, *fill*, etc.: *recall*, *refill*, *pitfall*, *sawmill*, and so on. Note, however, the spelling of *annul*, *enrol*, and *enthral* (compare *null*, *roll* and *thrall*). Note also the spelling of *fulfil*.

In all other cases, the word will end in a single *l*:

appeal	initial	sandal	trail
appal	instil	soil	trial
distil	model	soul	wool
equal	prevail	symbol	

Exception The only common exception is *install*, but this may also be spelt with a single *l*.

l becomes *ll*

For the rules governing the doubling of a single final *l* before a suffix (as in *controlling*, *distillation* and so on), see **doubling of final consonants.**

ll becomes *l*

A final double *l* drops one *l* before a suffix beginning with a consonant:

dull + *ly* = *dully*
full + *ly* = *fully*
full + *some* = *fulsome*

install + *ment* = *instalment*
skill + *ful* = *skilful*
thrall + *dom* = *thraldom*
will + *ful* = *wilful*
smell, spell, spill + *t* = *smelt, spelt, spilt*

Exception The suffix *-ness* is an exception to this rule:
dull + *ness* = *dullness*
ill + *ness* = *illness*

A few other words show similar changes. The spelling of the following should be noted:
all : *almighty, almost, already, altogether*
(but see also the chapter *One word or two?*)
bell : *belfry*
chill : *chilblain*
well : *welfare*

-ful or *full*?

For the difference between *two bagfuls* and *two bags full*, see chapter 3, *One word or two?*

-ly

Adverbs are generally formed by adding **-ly** to an adjective:
foolish : *foolishly*   *surprising* : *surprisingly*
initial : *initially*   *careful* : *carefully*
strange : *strangely*   *free* : *freely*

Certain categories of words are, however, exceptions to this rule:

1. Adjectives ending in *-ic* add *-ally* to form adverbs:
basic : *basically*   *economic* : *economically*
historic : *historically*

Exceptions *Politic* and *public* are the only adjectives ending in *ic* which add *-ly* rather than *-ally* to form adverbs:
Publically is a common error, *publicly* is the correct form.
Politicly is the adverb corresponding to the adjective *politic* (= 'wise', 'sensible'), while the adverb based on the adjective *political* is *politically*.

2. Adjectives ending in *-le* preceded by one or more consonants generally drop the *e* and add *y*:

simple : *simply*   *subtle* : *subtly*
single : *singly*   *double* : *doubly*
supple : *supply* (some people allow *supplely*)

3. *True, due, eerie* and *whole* drop their final *e* before adding *-ly*:

truly; duly; eerily; wholly

4. Adjectives ending in *y* preceded by a consonant alter this *y* to *i* before *-ly*:

silly : *sillily*   *weary* : *wearily*

Exceptions   Certain short adjectives ending in a *y* which is pronounced [ī] may have either *y* or *i* before *-ly*:

dry : *drily* or *dryly*
shy : *shily* or *shyly*
sly : *slily* or *slyly*

Only *spryly* and *wryly* are correct, however, not *sprily* or *wrily*.

If the *y* is preceded by a vowel, it does not change to *i* before *-ly*:

coy : *coyly*

Exceptions   Adjectives ending in *-ey* which are formed from nouns change the *ey* to *i* before *-ly* is added:

mate :   *matey* :   *matily*
dice :   *dicey* :   *dicily*

Gay has a corresponding adverb *gaily*. Note also the spelling of *daily*.

5. If an adjective ends in a double *l*, the corresponding adverb ends in *-lly*:

dull : *dully*   *shrill* : *shrilly*
full : *fully*

nouns

For the formation of plural nouns ⇒ **-s, -es**; **-os, -oes**; **-x, -s**; and **-y.**

-oes, -os see **-os, -oes.**

-or, -er, -ar see **-er, -or, -ar.**

-or, -our
The rules for choosing between **-or**, **-er** and **-ar** for agent nouns (i.e. 'doer' words like *swimmer* or *actor*) are given in the entry **-er, -or, -ar.** As far as choosing between **-or** and **-our** is concerned, you need only remember that all such 'doer' words end in **-or**, with the sole exception of **saviour.**

There are a number of words which end in **-our** in English. Many of these refer to abstract nouns (i.e. ideas and feelings) rather than to objects and things:

ardour	*favour*	*humour*	*rumour*
behaviour	*fervour*	*labour*	*savour*
candour	*flavour*	*misdemeanour*	*splendour*
clamour	*glamour*	*odour*	*valour*
colour	*honour*	*rigour*	*vigour*
endeavour			

Other common **-our** words are:

armour	*neighbour*	*tumour*
harbour	*parlour*	*vapour*

(Note that in American English, all the words in the above list are written with **-or**, not **-our**, with the exception of *glamour* which is commoner in the U.S. than *glamor*.)

Abstract words ending in **-or** are:

error	*pallor*	*stupor*	*torpor*
horror	*squalor*	*tenor*	*tremor*
languor			

Three other common **-or** words are *anchor*, *liquor*, and *mirror*.

dropping the *u*
When certain suffixes (i.e. 'word-endings') are added to **-our**

words, the *u* is dropped. This applied to the suffixes *-ary*, *-ation*, *-ial*, *-iferous*, *-ific*, *-ious*, *-ise/-ize*, and *-ous*:

honour	:	honorary	colour	:	coloration
armour	:	armorial	odour	:	odoriferous
honour	:	honorific	labour	:	laborious
glamour	:	glamorize	humour	:	humorous

Before other suffixes, the *u* is retained:

honour	:	honourable	labour	:	labourer
colour	:	colourful	favour	:	favourite
humour	:	humourless	armour	:	armoury
savour	:	savoury			

-ory, -ary, -ery see -ary, -ery, -ory.

-os, -oes

nouns

Nouns ending in *o* add either *es* or *s* alone in the plural.

Nouns which end in *oo*, or in which the final *o* is preceded by another vowel, add *s*:

zoos; embryos; radios; studios.

Of the other nouns ending in *o*, most add *s*, but the relatively small group of *es* words includes most of the commonest of the words which end in *o*. If we take *s* as the rule, we can then list the *es* plurals as exceptions. They are as follows:

buffaloes	embargoes	mangoes	tomatoes
cargoes	goes	mottoes	tornadoes
dingoes	heroes	Negroes	torpedoes
dominoes	hoboes	noes	vetoes
echoes	lingoes	potatoes	volcanoes

A number of words may be spelt with either *s* or *es*:

archipelago(e)s	flamingo(e)s	manifesto(e)s	portico(e)s
banjo(e)s	grotto(e)s	memento(e)s	salvo(e)s
dado(e)s	halo(e)s	mosquito(e)s	virago(e)s
desperado(e)s	innuendo(e)s	peccadillo(e)s	zero(e)s
fiasco(e)s	lasso(e)s		

Note The plural of *do* is *do's* or *dos* (as in *do's and don'ts*).

122

verbs

Compared to the nouns category, there are relatively few verbs which end in *o*, most of them (e.g. *lasso, radio, shampoo, video*) being words which can serve as both nouns and verbs. In the formation of the third person singular of the present tense (e.g. *he goes, she tangoes*), either *es* or *s* may be added, but the rule is very simple:

    if the noun adds *-es*, add *-es* in the verb;

    if it doesn't, or if there is no related noun, add *-s*;

    if the noun plural allows both *-es* and *-s* forms, add *-es* in the verb.

Exception There is only one exception, and that is *does*, which must never be written *dos*.

-our, -or see -or, -our.

-ous, -us

There should be little confusion between these two endings once it is realized that **-ous** is an *adjective* ending and **-us** a *noun* ending:

famous	*anonymous*	*enormous*	*covetous*
impetuous	*spacious*	*poisonous*	*cancerous*
abacus	*thesaurus*	*impetus*	*circus*
virus	*lotus*	*cactus*	*octopus*

Exceptions Words taken directly from Latin, in which many adjectives end in *-us*, do not follow this rule. One such exception is *emeritus*.

plurals

For the formation of plural nouns, see the articles **-s, -es**; **-os, -oes**; **-x, -s**; and **-y.**

-s, -es

nouns

To form a plural noun, it is generally sufficient to add *s* to the singular noun:

car	: *cars*	*table*	: *tables*
book	: *books*	*alibi*	: *alibis*

The following special rules should be noted:

1. If a noun ends in *s, z, x, sh* or *ch* (when pronounced [*ch*]), add *es* to the singular to form the plural:

kiss	: *kisses*	*waltz*	: *waltzes*
box	: *boxes*	*bush*	: *bushes*
church	: *churches*		

Note If the final *ch* is not pronounced [*ch*], add *s* alone:

loch : *lochs*   *stomach* : *stomachs*

2. Most words ending in *o* add *s* but some add *es*: see the entry **-os, -oes** where this is treated in detail.

3. Words ending in a consonant followed by *y* normally add *es*, and the *y* becomes *i*:

fly : *flies*   *entry* : *entries*

Exception The plural of *poly* (short for 'polytechnic') is *polys*.

Words ending in *y* preceded by a vowel simply add *s*:

boy : *boys*   *day* : *days*

See the entry **-y** for more details.

4. A number of nouns double their final consonant when *es* is added:

quiz : *quizzes*   *fiz* : *fizzes*

This follows the rules given in the article **doubling of final consonants.**

Exceptions The following words are, or in some cases may optionally be, spelt with a single letter where a doubled consonant would be expected according to the general rule:

bus	: plural	*buses* (rarely *busses)*
gas	: plural	*gases*
plus	: plural	*pluses* or *plusses*
yes	: plural	*yeses* or *yesses*

5. Plural nouns should not normally be written with apostrophes: *spy's, radio's, bag's of stick's* are all wrong. But see the article **apostrophe** for examples of apostrophes correctly used in the formation of plurals.

6. A number of plurals are irregular:

analysis : *analyses* *knife* : *knives*
index : *indices* *species* : *species*

In such cases, however, the written form of the words are predictable from their pronunciation, and the spelling should therefore present no problems.

7. In words of French origin which end in a silent *s* (e.g. *chassis*, *corps*, *fracas*, *rendezvous*), the plural is identical in form to the singular but the *s* is pronounced: *two chassis*, not *two chassises*.

For words of French origin that can take *-x* or *-s* in the plural ⟹ **-x, -s**.

verbs
The rules for forming the third person singular of the present tense (e.g. *he stays, she lies*) are virtually the same as those for the formation of plural nouns given above:

bring : *brings* *make* : *makes*
kiss : *kisses* *fix* : *fixes*
stay : *stays* *cry* : *cries*

See again the articles **-os, -oes; -y**; and **doubling of final consonants** for problem areas.

Warning One minor difference between plural noun formation and that of the *-es* verb-form is found in the words of French origin which end in a silent *s*. Although nothing is added in the plural noun, *es* is added in the verb:

two rendezvous but *he rendezvouses with them* (the two words being pronounced the same although spelt differently).

One other difference to note is that the plural of the noun *taxi* is *taxis*, but the 3rd person singular of the present tense of the verb is *taxies*.

-se, -ce see **-ce, -se.**

-sede, -cede, -ceed see **-cede, -ceed, -sede.**

-sion, -tion see **-tion, -sion, -cion.**

-sy, -cy see **-acy, -asy.**

-tch, -ch see **-ch, -tch.**

-tion, -sion, -cion

To many people, there seems to be no rhyme or reason to the spelling of words like *intention* and *extension*, or *distinction*, *coercion*, and *diversion*. How is one to know when to write *t*, when *c*, and when *s*?

Actually the situation is not as hopeless as might at first appear. There are some very clear guidelines to follow, and only a small number of words that should cause any problems at all.

-cion
There are only two common words which end in *-cion*:

    coercion   *suspicion*

Warning Do not forget that there are a large number of words which end in *-cian*, e.g.:

    magician   *musician*   *politician*
    mathematician   *optician*   *technician*

Notice that these are all jobs which describe a person's job or occupation, and that most of them are related to words ending in *-ic*, *-ics*, or *-ical*:

    magic : *magician*   *politics* : *politician*
    technical : *technician*

-tion, -sion
To sort out the rules governing the spelling of words ending in **-tion** and **-sion**, it is helpful to divide up the words according to whether the ending follows a vowel or a consonant.

    1. *-tion* and *-sion* after a vowel
If the ending is pronounced [*zhən*], it will be written *-sion*:

    adhesion   *decision*   *fusion*   *persuasion*
    confusion   *devision*   *incision*   *vision*

If the ending is pronounced [shən], it will almost always be written *-tion*:

addition	notion	ration	station
nation	position	solution	taxation

and also the large group of words ending in *-ation* which are formed from words which end in *-ate*:

create : creation   meditate: meditation
educate : education   rotate   : rotation

Exceptions There are a number of words which end in [shən], spelt *-ssion*. These words are easily identifiable in that they are based on words ending in *ss* or on words ending in *-mit* or *-cede*, or are at least clearly related to words spelt with a double *s*:

discuss : discussion   permit   : permission
admit   : admission   concede : concession
accede : accession   obsessive : obsession
possess : possession

Note also *mission*, *passion*, and *session*.

2. *-tion* and *-sion* after a consonant

After any consonant except *l*, *n* and *r*, the spelling is *-tion*:

action   infection   suggestion
deception   option

Note A few words end in *-xion*. See **-ction, -xion** for notes on these.

After *l*, the ending is *-sion*:

emulsion   expulsion   propulsion

After *n* and *r*, the situation is more confusing. In general, words related to or based on words which end in *t* or *-tain* are spelt *-tion*, and those related to or based on words ending in *d* or *se* are spelt *-sion*:

abort	: abortion	exert	: exertion
assert	: assertion	extort	: extortion
distort	: distortion	invent	: invention
abstain	: abstention	retain	: retention

ascend	: ascension	expand	: expansion
comprehend	: comprehension	extend	: extension
averse	: aversion	immerse	: immersion

Exceptions *Attention*, *contention*, and *intention* have a *t* where by the above rule *s* would be expected, and *conversion*, *diversion*, *extraversion* and *introversion* have *s* where *t* would be expected (notice that these are all related to words ending in *-vert*).

residual problems

The following words are spelt with *t*:

mention	portion	proportion

These words are spelt with *s*:

aspersion	incursion	recursion	tension
dimension	mansion	scansion	version
excursion	pension		

-x, -s

Words of French origin ending in *-eu* and *-eau*, which regularly take an *x* in the plural in French, usually do so also in English, although the regular English plural ending *s* is also correct in most cases:

adieu	:	*adieux* or *adieus*
beau	:	*beaux*
bureau	:	*bureaux* or *bureaus*
château	:	*châteaux*
gâteau	:	*gâteaux* or *gâteaus*
milieu	:	*milieux* or *milieus*
plateau	:	*plateaux* or *plateaus*
portmanteau	:	*portmanteaux* or *portmanteaus*
tableau	:	*tableaux*
trousseau	:	*trousseaux* or *trousseaus*

-xion, -ction see -ction, -xion.

-us, -ous see -ous, -us.

verbs

For the formation of the past tense and past participle of regular verbs ⇒ **-ed, -d**.

For the formation of the present participle ⇒ **-ing**.

Also ⇒ **doubling of final consonants; -e; -c; -os, -oes**; and **-y**.

-y

nouns

If the final *y* of a noun is preceded by a consonant, the plural will end in *-ies*:

cry : *cries*   *lady* : *ladies*
nationality : *nationalities*

Exceptions   Note the following exceptions:

1. Proper names are an exception to this rule: *the two Germanys*; *the four Marys*. Note, however, that historians refer to *the Kingdom of the Two Sicilies*.

2. The plural of *poly* (= polytechnic) is *polys*.

3. Compound nouns in which the *y* is part of an adverb or preposition are a further exception to the rule:
stand-bys   *lay-bys*

If the final *y* is preceded by a vowel, *s* alone is added to form the plural:

day : *days*   *buoy* : *buoys*
monkey : *monkeys*

Exception   Note that the (rather rare) plural of *money* may be either *moneys* or *monies*.

Note   A *u* following a *q* is pronounced [*w*] and counts as a consonant:

soliloquy : *soliloquies*

verbs

Verbs follow essentially the same pattern of construction as nouns. If the final *y* of a verb is preceded by a consonant, the 3rd person singular of the present tense will end in *-ies* (*he cries*, *she flies*) and the past tense will end in *-ied* (*they cried*). If the *y* is preceded by a vowel, *s* alone is added in the present tense and *ed* in the past tense:

convey, conveys, conveyed
stay, stays, stayed

Exceptions *Said, laid, paid* are exceptions to this rule.

The same rule applies to the final *y* of verbs when other suffixes (or 'word-endings') are added:

vary	:	*variable*	*enjoy*	: *enjoyable*
ally	:	*alliance*	*annoy*	: *annoyance*
carry	:	*carrier*	*employ*	: *employer*
try	:	*trial*	*betray*	: *betrayal*

and so on.

Note, however, that *y* does not change to *i* before an *i*:

vary : *varying*   *carry* : *carrying*

Exceptions A number of one-syllable verbs in which the *y* is pronounced [ī] are exceptions or partial exceptions to this rule when *er* is added:

dry : *dryer* or *drier*
fly : *flyer* or *flier*
fry : *fryer* or *frier*

but only *trier* is correct.

Note also the spelling of *flyable*.

adjectives

A number of common adjectives are formed from nouns by the addition of *y*:

meat : *meaty*   *shadow* : *shadowy*

Such adjectives follow the general rules for doubling of consonants, dropping of final *e*'s, and adding *k* to final *c*'s:

grit	:	*gritty*	*bone*	:	*bony*
pal	:	*pally*	*ice*	:	*icy*
sag	:	*saggy*	*noise*	:	*noisy*
panic	:	*panicky*			

Exceptions   The following exceptions should be noted:

i) The final *e* is retained in words that end in *ue*, and also unpredictably in a small number of other words:

glue : *gluey*   *mate* : *matey*
cage : *cagey*   *pace* : *pacey*
dice : *dicey*   *price* : *pricey*
and *holey* (= full of holes), in contrast to *holy* (= sacred).
Both *nosy* and *nosey* are correct.

ii) When the base noun ends in *y*, *-ey* rather than *y* alone is added:

clay : *clayey*
-ey is also added to *goo* to form *gooey*, and note also the spelling of *phoney*.

comparative and superlative adjectives
To form the comparatives and superlatives of adjectives ending in a *y* preceded by a consonant, change the *y* to *i* and add *-er* and *-est*:

silly : *sillier* : *silliest*
happy : *happier* : *happiest*

Exceptions   Again some one-syllable words in which the *y* is pronounced [ī] are exceptions, or partial exceptions, to this rule:

shy : *shyer/shyest*   or *shier/shiest*
sly : *slyer/slyest*   or *slier/sliest*
wry : *wryer/wryest* or *wrier/wriest*
but only *drier/driest* and *spryer/spryest* are correct.

Adjectives in which the *y* is preceded by a vowel retain the *y*:

grey : *greyer* : *greyest*

Exceptions   A group of exceptions are those adjectives ending in *-ey* listed above (e.g. *clayey*, *matey*, *gooey*, *pricey*). In such words, the *-ey* changes to *i*:

pricey : *pricier* : *priciest*

other suffixes

The same rules apply before other word-endings:

happy : *happily*	*coy* : *coyly*
happy : *happiness*	*coy* : *coyness*
merry : *merriment*	
forty : *fortieth*	

and so on. As with verb-derivatives, a final *y* does not change to *i* before an *i*: *prettyish, fortyish.*

Exceptions There are a number of exceptions:

i) *dryly/drily, shyly/shily, slyly/slily* are correct, but only *spryly* and *wryly; dryness, shyness, slyness, spryness, wryness* (not *driness* etc.);

ii) *cagily, matily,* etc., but the nouns in *-ness* pose a slight problem, as according to most authorities some of the *-ey* adjectives change the *ey* to *i* before *-ness* while others do not, and the authorities do not agree on which words belong to which category. Faced with this area of uncertainty, it seems simpler to adopt a straightforward rule and always change *ey* to *i* when the *y* is preceded by a consonant, and not when it is preceded by a vowel:

matey : *matiness*	*clayey* : *clayiness*
gluey : *glueyness*	*gooey* : *gooeyness*

iii) note *gaily,* and also *daily;*

iv) The noun from *busy* is *busyness* [*biz′inəs*], to distinguish this word from *business* [*biz′nəs*].

-y, -ie

The great majority of English words ending in [*i*] are spelt with a *y*, e.g.:

berry	*dairy*	*library*	*poppy*
angry	*cheery*	*happy*	*silly*
carry	*dally*	*marry*	*scurry*

Certain nouns, however, end in *-ie*:

1. Some shortened forms of words:

bookie	(= book-maker)	*mountie*
budgie	(= budgerigar)	*movie*
goalie		*nightie*

2. Diminutives, especially those used in speaking to young children, and terms of endearment:

birdie	*doggie*	*laddie*
chappie	*fishie*	*lassie*
dearie	*horsie*	

Spelling note   Notice the difference in spelling between these nouns and similar or related adjectives which end in *y*:

a fishy smell
a rather horsy face

3. Certain other nouns:

brownie	*genie*	*quickie*
cookie	*kiltie*	*walkie-talkie*
coolie	*oldie*	

Some words may be spelt with either *-ie* or *-y*:

caddie/caddy (in golf, but only *tea-caddy* is correct)

ghillie/gillie/gilly	*pixie/pixy*
girlie/girly	*rookie/rooky*
hippie/hippy	*softie/softy*
junkie/junky	

In all cases. the forms in *-ie* are the commoner.

Warning   Do not confuse these three words:

bogey (= the score in golf fixed as a standard for a good player)

bogie (= a low truck or undercarriage on a locomotive)

bogy (= a goblin or bugbear; may also be written *bogey*)

5.

Beginnings, Middles and Endings

One way of learning to spell correctly is to split words up into their component parts and to check that each part is correctly spelt. Many English words, particularly those of Latin and Greek origin, are composed of elements the spelling of which is consistently the same in all the words in which the elements appear. Learning to recognize each element at the beginning, in the middle, or at the end of a word is therefore a very useful spelling-aid.

The following list provides examples of some of the most frequent 'combining-elements' in English, along with an approximate description of the meanings they carry:

aer(o)	(air, aircraft)	*aeroplane, aerodrome, aeronautical, aerobics, aerial*
agr(o)	(field, farming)	*agrarian, agriculture, agrochemical*
algia	(pain)	*neuralgia*
ambi	(both)	*ambidextrous, ambivalent*
ante	(before)	*antenatal, anteroom*
anthrop(o)	(man, mankind)	*anthropoid, anthropology, philanthropy*
anti	(against)	*anti-aircraft, antifreeze*
aqua	(water)	*aquatic, aqualung, aquarium*
arch(ae)(o)	(old)	*archaic, archaeology*
astro	(star)	*astronomy, astrophysics*
audio	(hearing)	*audio-visual*
auto	(self)	*autobiography, automobile*
bi	(two)	*biannual, bicycle*
biblio	(book)	*bibliography*
bio	(life)	*biography, biology*
cardi(o)	(heart)	*cardiac, cardiology*
carn	(flesh)	*carnivorous*

cata	(down)	*catastrophe, catarrh*
cent(i)	(one hundred)	*century, centigrade, centipede*
	(one hundredth)	*centimetre, centilitre*
chron(o)	(time)	*chronic, chronology*
cid(e)	(killing, killer)	*homicide, fratricidal*
crat, cracy	(ruler, rule)	*democrat, aristocracy*
crypt(o)	(hidden)	*cryptogram, crypto-Communist*
deca	(ten)	*decade*
deci	(one tenth)	*decilitre*
dexter, dextr	(right)	*dexterity, ambidextrous*
dia	(across, through)	*diagonal, diameter, diarrhoea*
dis	(not)	*dissatisfaction*
dox	(opinion)	*orthodox, orthodoxy*
duct	(lead)	*conduct, deduction*
dys	(badly)	*dyslexia, dyspepsia*
equ(i)	(equal)	*equidistance, equal*
fore	(before)	*foretell*
frater, fratr	(brother)	*fraternal, fratricide*
gam(y)	(marriage)	*bigamy, polygamy*
ge(o)	(Earth)	*geography, geology*
gram, graph(y)	(write)	*diagram, autograph, biography, telegram, seismograph*
gyn(o), gynaec(o)	(woman)	*gynaecology, misogynist*
haem(o)	(blood)	*haemophiliac, haemorrhage*
hect(o)	(one hundred)	*hectare, hectolitre*
hepta	(seven)	*heptagon*
heter(o)	(opposite)	*heterosexual*
hexa	(eight)	*hexagon*
homo	(same)	*homosexual, homogeneous*
hydr(o)	(water)	*hydraulic, hydro-electric*
hyper	(beyond, too much)	*hyper-active*
hypo	(under)	*hypodermic*
iatr	(doctor, medicine)	*psychiatry, geriatrics*

iso	(equal)	*isobar, isotype*
itis	(disease, inflammation)	*bronchitis*
kilo	(one thousand)	*kilogram*
logy	(study of)	*geology, biology, zoology*
mater, matr	(mother)	*maternal, matricide*
micro	(small)	*microphone, microscope*
milli	(one thousandth)	*millimetre*
mis	(wrongly)	*mislead, misinform, misspell*
mono	(single)	*monologue, monolithic*
mort	(death)	*mortal*
naut	(sailor, sailing)	*astronaut, nautical*
neo	(new)	*Neolithic, neologism*
neur(o)	(nerves)	*neuralgia, neurology*
oct(o)	(eight)	*octet, octagonal, octopus*
omni	(all)	*omnipotent, omnivorous*
ortho	(straight, correct)	*orthodox, orthopaedics*
osis	(disease)	*silicosis, psychosis*
paed(o)	(child)	*orthopaedics, paediatrician*
pater, patr	(father)	*paternal, patricide*
phil, phile	(loving)	*philanthropy, Francophilia, Francophile*
phob(e)	(fear, hatred)	*phobia, Anglophobic*
phon, phone	(sound)	*telephone, microphone, phonetic*
poly	(many)	*polygamous, polytechnic*
pseudo	(false)	*pseudonym*
psych(o)	(mind)	*psychiatry, psychology, psychic*
quadr(i)	(four)	*quadrangle, quadrilateral*
quasi	(only apparently)	*quasi-scientific*
retro	(backwards)	*retrogression*
rrh	(flowing)	*diarrhoea, haemorrhage, catarrh*
rupt	(break)	*disrupt, interrupt, rupture*
sci	(know)	*science, conscience, omniscient*
scop(e)	(viewing)	*microscope, telescope, stereoscopic*

sect	(cut)	*bisect, section, sector, insect*
semi	(half)	*semi-circle*
stereo	(solid, three-dimensional)	*stereoscopic*
tele	(far)	*telephone, television*
tetra	(four)	*tetrahedron*
the(o)	(god)	*theology, atheism*
therm(o)	(heat)	*thermal, thermodynamics*
tri	(three)	*triangle*
vis	(seeing)	*visible, television*
vor	(eating)	*carnivore, carnivorous, insectivorous, voracious*

6.

How to Find a Word You Cannot Spell

One problem that poor spellers are constantly faced with is how to find a word in a dictionary or in a book such as this when they do not know how to spell it in the first place. For example, someone who does not realize that there is a 'silent' *p* at the beginning of *pneumonia* or *psychology* is going to have a long and fruitless search if he or she hunts for the correct spelling of these words under *n* or *s*. Even where there are no silent letters to complicate matters, the rules of English spelling will often allow several conceivable spellings of a word, not all of which will necessarily occur to someone who is searching for the correct one: it would, for example, be pointless to search for *physical* under *f*, *xylophone* under *z*, or *ewe* under *y*.

To help overcome this difficulty, this chapter comprises a list of alternative spellings for various English sounds. If you have searched for a word in a dictionary or word-list and failed to find it where you expected it to be, consult the lists below, and try looking under some of the other spellings suggested in it. The table is particularly helpful in that it indicates the 'silent' letters which cause so many problems for poor spellers.

Sound	Possible Spelling	Examples
b	b	*book, rub*
	bb	*babble, flabby*
p	p	*pin, sip*
	pp	*apple, nipped*
	ph	*shepherd*
d	d	*dry, body, cold*
	dd	*cuddle, add*
	ed	*called*
	ld	*could, would, should*

t	t	*tin, not, spilt*
	tt	*better, kettle*
	th	*Thomas, thyme*
	ed	*walked*
	pt	*pterodactyl, receipt*
	bt	*doubt, debt, redoubtable*
	ct	*indict, victuals*
	ght	*taught*
g	g	*big, get*
	gg	*bigger, begging, egg, aggravate*
	gh	*ghost, aghast*
	gu	*guard, guarantee, vague*
	x	*example* (x = [*gz*])
k	k	*key, break*
	c	*can, panic, sceptic*
	ck	*back, cackle, panicky*
	cc	*tobacco, account*
	q(u)	*quite, cheque, liquor*
	ch	*character, school*
	cq(u)	*acquire, lacquer*
	cch	*saccharine*
	lk	*folk, talk*
	kh	*khaki*
	x	*extra* (x = [*ks*]), *luxury* (x = [*ksh*])
m	m	*me, mime, lump*
	mm	*common*
	mn	*solemn*
	mb	*bomb*
	lm	*calm*
	gm	*paradigm*
	chm	*drachm*
	nm	*government*

n	n	*not, sun*
	nn	*sunny*
	kn	*knot, knit*
	gn	*gnat*
	pn	*pneumonia*
	mn	*mnemonic*
ng	ng	*sing, longing*
	ngue	*tongue*
	n	*plank, sink, hankie, finger*
	nd	*handkerchief*
f	f	*finger, if, soft*
	ff	*off, sniff, coffee*
	ph	*physical, photograph*
	gh	*cough, enough*
	lf	*half, calf*
	ft	*often, soften*
v	v	*van, sieve, shiver*
	vv	*navvy*
	f	*of*
	ph	*Stephen*
s	s	*sit, books*
	ss	*mess*
	c	*city, cynic, mice*
	sc	*scent, scene, fascinate*
	ps	*psychology*
	st	*fasten, castle*
	sc	*muscle*
	sw	*sword*
	sch	*schism*
z	z	*zero, fez*
	zz	*puzzle, fizzy*
	ss	*scissors*
	s	*frogs, churches, was, cheese*
	x	*xylophone*

ch	ch	*church, cheese*
	tch	*match, watch*
	t	*question, future, righteous*
	c	*cello*
	cz	*Czech*
j	j	*judge*
	dg(e)	*judge, judg(e)ment*
	g(e)	*age, gem*
	gg	*exaggerate*
	dj	*adjust*
	d	*soldier, graduate*
sh	sh	*sheep, fish, fashion*
	ch	*chivalry, machine*
	s	*sure, tension*
	ss	*mission*
	sc	*fascist, conscience*
	c	*ocean, special*
	sch	*schist, fuchsia*
	t	*attention*
zh	s	*pleasure, vision, unusual*
	z	*seizure, azure*
	ge	*rouge*
th	th	*thin, tooth*
dh	th	*then, smooth, rhythm*
w	w	*wet, worn*
	u	*quiet*
	o	*choir, one*
	wh	*when, whether*
y	y	*yet, youth*
	j	*hallelujah*
	i	*opinion*

(yoo)	ew	*ewe, few, view*
	u(e)	*use, queue, cue*
	eu	*feud, pseudo*
	eau	*beauty*
r	r	*red, fur, pretty*
	rr	*furry, purring*
	wr	*wrong, write*
	rh	*rhyme, rhythm*
	rrh	*diarrhoea, haemorrhage*
h	h	*hot*
	wh	*who*
l	l	*lead, pilfer, spilt, bottle, medal*
	ll	*hell, calling, gorilla*
a/ä	a	*hat, car, father, black, castle, path, shah*
	au	*laugh*
	al	*half, calf*
	ea	*heart*
	e	*clerk, sergeant*
	aa	*bazaar*
	ai	*plaid*
	i	*meringue*
ā	ay	*pay, say, prayer*
	ai	*paid, straight, hair*
	a – e	*make, take, age, hare*
	ea	*break, pear*
	ao	*gaol*
	au	*gauge*
	ei	*vein, freight, reign, their*
	ey	*they, prey*
	e – e	*where*
	é(e)	*café, fiancée*
	ae	*Gaelic, aeroplane*

e	e	*bed, better, berry*
	ea	*bread, instead, pleasure*
	ai	*said*
	ay	*says*
	a	*many, any*
	eo	*leopard*
	ei	*leisure, heifer*
	ie	*friend*
	ae	*aesthetic*
ē	ee	*sheep, beer*
	ea	*team, appear, please*
	e – e	*scene, mere*
	e	*equal*
	ie	*field, fierce*
	ei	*weird, ceiling*
	ey	*key*
	eo	*people*
	oe	*amoeba, phoenix*
	i	*police, souvenir*
	ay	*quay*
	ae	*Caesar*
i	i	*hit, build, guilt, infinite*
	y	*hymn, tyranny*
	a	*accurate, marriage*
	ie	*sieve*
	ei	*foreign*
	ai	*mountain*
	o	*women*
	u	*busy, business*
	e	*English*
ī	ie	*pie, fiery*
	i – e	*bite, fire, ice*
	(e)igh	*fight, height*
	y	*try, buy, dye, tyrant*

	i	*tried, isle*
	ai	*aisle*
o/ö	o	*pot, rotten, John, order*
	ou	*cough, brought*
	a	*watch, yacht*
	au	*caught*
	aw	*draw*
ō/ö	o	*sport, open*
	o – e	*bore, wrote, owe*
	oa	*soap, broad, load*
	oe	*toe*
	oo	*brooch, floor*
	ou	*soul, four, though*
	ow	*grow*
	ew	*sew*
	ol	*folk*
	eau	*eau de Cologne, beau*
	au	*mauve*
	eo	*yeoman*
ōō/ŏŏ	oo	*food, pool, troop, good*
	u	*pull, sure, truth, rude*
	ue	*blue, true*
	ou	*group, troupe, through, tour, would*
	o – e	*move*
	oe	*shoe*
	o	*wolf*
	ew	*few, flew*
	(o)eu	*rheumatism, manoeuvre*
	ui	*fruit*
ow	ow	*now, power*
	ou	*ounce, our, plough, mouse*
	au	*sauerkraut*

oi	oy	*boy, buoy*
	oi	*poison*
u	u	*cut, button*
	oo	*blood*
	ou	*trouble, young*
	o	*son, come, tongue, does*
û	ear	*heard*
	er(r)	*her, fertile, err*
	ere	*were*
	eur	*chauffeur*
	ir	*bird*
	o(u)r	*word, journey*
	ur(r)	*church, purr*
	yr	*myrtle*
	olo	*colonel*

Remember also the silent *h* at the beginning of words such as *heir*, *hour* and *honour*—if you cannot find a word that you think begins with a vowel, it might be worth looking under *h*.

7.

American Spelling

There are a number of differences between the spelling of words in American English and that of British English. Some of the most important of these are listed below:

1. Some verbs ending in *l* and *p* which in British English double their final consonant before *-ing*, *-ed* and *-er/-or* do not do so in American English: for example, British English *travelling*, *kidnapped*, *equalled*, *counsellor*, but American *traveling*, *kidnaped*, *equaled*, *counselor*. This difference applies to certain nouns and adjectives also: note for example the normal American spellings *carburetor* (British *carburettor*) and *woolen* (British *woollen*). Notice that the American spellings of the words conform to the general rules for doubling or non-doubling of final consonants outlined in the entry **doubling of final consonants** in chapter 4, whereas the British spellings are exceptions to the rules.

2. With verbs that may be spelt *-ise* or *-ize*, Americans prefer *-ize*.

3. Most words which in British English end in *-our* end in *-or* in American English, e.g. *color*, *humor*. *Saviour* and *glamour* are exceptions.

4. Many words which in British English end in *-re* are spelt *-er* by Americans: *center*, *theater*, *fiber*, *specter*, *meager*. Exceptions to this are generally words ending in *-cre* or *-gre*: *acre*, *massacre*, *ogre* are correct in both British and American English.

5. The tendency to replace *ae* and *oe* in words from Greek and Latin by *e* is more strongly developed in the United States than in Britain: *aetiology*, *haemoglobin*, *encyclopaedia*, *diarrhoea*, *oesophagus* are normal in British

English, *etiology*, *hemoglobin*, *encyclopedia*, *diarrhea*, and *esophagus* usual in American English.

6. Among the other words which are spelt differently in American English are *axe* (Amer. *ax*), *catalogue* (Amer. *catalog*), *cheque* (Amer. *check*), *plough* (Amer. *plow*), *programme* (Amer. *program*), *sceptic* (Amer. *skeptic*), *tyre* (Amer. *tire*).